50 American Breakfast Food Recipes for Home

By: Kelly Johnson

Table of Contents

- Pancakes
- Waffles
- French toast
- Scrambled eggs
- Omelette
- Eggs Benedict
- Breakfast burrito
- Breakfast sandwich
- Bagels with cream cheese
- Breakfast potatoes
- Hash browns
- Breakfast sausage
- Bacon
- Biscuits and gravy
- Corned beef hash
- Cinnamon rolls
- Quiche
- Breakfast pizza
- Breakfast tacos
- Granola with yogurt and fruit
- Muffins (various flavors)
- Doughnuts
- Fruit salad
- Smoothies
- Crepes
- Breakfast casserole
- English muffins with jam
- Breakfast quesadilla
- Scones
- Huevos rancheros
- Grits
- Sausage gravy and biscuits
- Blueberry pancakes
- Banana bread
- Frittata

- Greek yogurt with honey and nuts
- Oatmeal with toppings
- Cinnamon toast
- Breakfast sliders
- Belgian waffles
- Breakfast wraps
- Breakfast strata
- Pancake skewers
- Breakfast BLT
- Breakfast pita
- Chilaquiles
- Avocado toast with eggs
- Breakfast flatbread
- Quinoa breakfast bowl
- Breakfast grilled cheese

Pancakes

Ingredients:

- 1 cup all-purpose flour
- 2 tablespoons sugar
- 1 teaspoon baking powder
- 1/2 teaspoon baking soda
- 1/4 teaspoon salt
- 1 cup buttermilk (or substitute with 1 cup milk mixed with 1 tablespoon vinegar or lemon juice)
- 1 large egg
- 2 tablespoons melted butter or vegetable oil
- 1 teaspoon vanilla extract (optional)

Instructions:

1. In a large bowl, whisk together the flour, sugar, baking powder, baking soda, and salt.
2. In another bowl, whisk together the buttermilk, egg, melted butter or oil, and vanilla extract (if using).
3. Pour the wet ingredients into the dry ingredients and stir until just combined. The batter should be slightly lumpy. Do not overmix.
4. Heat a non-stick skillet or griddle over medium heat. Lightly grease with butter or oil.
5. Pour about 1/4 cup of batter onto the skillet for each pancake. Cook until bubbles form on the surface and the edges look set, about 2-3 minutes.
6. Flip the pancakes and cook until golden brown on the other side, about 1-2 minutes more.
7. Repeat with the remaining batter, greasing the skillet as needed.

Serve pancakes warm with butter, maple syrup, fruit, whipped cream, or any other toppings of your choice. Enjoy your homemade pancakes!

Waffles

Ingredients:

- 1 3/4 cups all-purpose flour
- 2 tablespoons sugar
- 1 tablespoon baking powder
- 1/2 teaspoon salt
- 2 large eggs
- 1 3/4 cups milk
- 1/2 cup vegetable oil or melted butter
- 1 teaspoon vanilla extract (optional)
- Cooking spray or additional oil/butter for greasing the waffle iron

Instructions:

1. Preheat your waffle iron according to manufacturer's instructions.
2. In a large bowl, whisk together the flour, sugar, baking powder, and salt.
3. In another bowl, beat the eggs. Add the milk, vegetable oil or melted butter, and vanilla extract (if using). Whisk until well combined.
4. Pour the wet ingredients into the dry ingredients and stir until just combined. The batter should be slightly lumpy. Do not overmix.
5. Lightly grease the preheated waffle iron with cooking spray, oil, or melted butter.
6. Pour enough batter onto the center of the waffle iron to cover about two-thirds of the surface area (amount will vary depending on your waffle iron size).
7. Close the lid and cook according to your waffle iron's instructions, usually until golden brown and crisp, about 4-5 minutes.
8. Carefully remove the waffle and repeat with the remaining batter.

Serve waffles warm with butter, maple syrup, fruit, whipped cream, or any other toppings you desire. Enjoy your homemade waffles!

French toast

Ingredients:

- 4 slices of bread (thick slices like Texas toast or challah work well)
- 2 large eggs
- 1/2 cup milk
- 1 tablespoon granulated sugar (optional, adjust to taste)
- 1/2 teaspoon vanilla extract
- 1/4 teaspoon ground cinnamon
- Butter or oil for cooking
- Toppings of your choice (maple syrup, powdered sugar, fresh fruit, etc.)

Instructions:

1. In a shallow bowl or pie plate, whisk together the eggs, milk, sugar (if using), vanilla extract, and ground cinnamon until well combined.
2. Heat a non-stick skillet or griddle over medium heat. Add a small amount of butter or oil to coat the pan.
3. Dip each slice of bread into the egg mixture, turning to coat both sides thoroughly. Let excess mixture drip off.
4. Place the coated bread slices onto the preheated skillet or griddle. Cook until golden brown on each side, about 2-3 minutes per side.
5. Remove the French toast from the skillet and repeat with the remaining slices of bread, adding more butter or oil to the skillet as needed.
6. Serve warm with your favorite toppings such as maple syrup, powdered sugar, fresh fruit, or whipped cream.

Enjoy your delicious homemade French toast!

Scrambled eggs

Ingredients:

- 4 large eggs
- Salt and pepper, to taste
- 2 tablespoons milk or cream (optional)
- 1 tablespoon butter or cooking oil

Instructions:

1. Crack the eggs into a bowl. Add salt, pepper, and milk or cream (if using).
2. Use a fork or whisk to beat the eggs until the yolks and whites are well combined and slightly frothy.
3. Heat a non-stick skillet over medium-low heat and add the butter or oil. Allow it to melt and coat the pan evenly.
4. Pour the beaten eggs into the skillet. Let them cook undisturbed for a few seconds until the edges start to set.
5. Gently stir the eggs with a spatula, pushing them from the edges towards the center. Continue cooking and stirring occasionally until the eggs are mostly set but still slightly creamy.
6. Remove the skillet from heat just before the eggs are fully cooked, as they will continue to cook from the residual heat.
7. Serve immediately while hot.

You can customize your scrambled eggs by adding ingredients like cheese, herbs, diced vegetables, or cooked meats. Enjoy your fluffy scrambled eggs for a hearty breakfast!

Omelette

Ingredients:

- 2-3 large eggs
- Salt and pepper, to taste
- 1 tablespoon butter or cooking oil
- Fillings of your choice (e.g., cheese, diced vegetables, cooked meats, herbs)

Instructions:

1. Crack the eggs into a bowl. Season with salt and pepper, and whisk until well combined.
2. Heat an 8-10 inch non-stick skillet over medium heat. Add the butter or oil and let it melt and coat the skillet evenly.
3. Pour the beaten eggs into the skillet. Let them cook undisturbed for a few seconds until the edges start to set.
4. Using a spatula, gently push the cooked edges towards the center of the skillet, tilting the skillet to let the uncooked eggs flow to the edges.
5. Continue cooking and gently lifting the edges of the omelette to allow the uncooked eggs to flow underneath. Cook until the eggs are mostly set but still slightly runny on top.
6. Sprinkle your desired fillings over one half of the omelette.
7. Carefully fold the omelette in half with the spatula. Press down gently to seal and cook for another 1-2 minutes until the fillings are heated through and the omelette is cooked to your liking.
8. Slide the omelette onto a plate and serve immediately.

You can garnish the omelette with additional toppings like fresh herbs, salsa, or sour cream if desired. Enjoy your delicious homemade omelette!

Eggs Benedict

Ingredients:

- 4 large eggs
- 2 English muffins, split and toasted
- 4 slices Canadian bacon or cooked ham
- Fresh chives or parsley, finely chopped (for garnish, optional)

For the Hollandaise Sauce:

- 3 large egg yolks
- 1 tablespoon lemon juice
- 1/2 cup unsalted butter, melted
- Pinch of salt
- Pinch of cayenne pepper or paprika (optional)

Instructions:

1. Poach the Eggs:

- Fill a large saucepan with water and bring it to a gentle simmer over medium heat.
- Crack each egg into a small bowl or cup.
- Carefully slide each egg into the simmering water, one at a time.
- Poach the eggs for about 3-4 minutes until the whites are set but the yolks are still runny.
- Remove the poached eggs with a slotted spoon and drain them on paper towels. Trim any ragged edges if desired.

2. Prepare the Hollandaise Sauce:

- In a heatproof bowl that fits snugly over the saucepan (or a double boiler), whisk together the egg yolks and lemon juice.
- Place the bowl over the saucepan of simmering water (make sure the water doesn't touch the bottom of the bowl).
- Continue whisking constantly until the mixture begins to thicken, about 2-3 minutes.
- Gradually drizzle in the melted butter, whisking constantly, until the sauce is smooth and thickened.
- Remove the bowl from heat and season the hollandaise sauce with salt and cayenne pepper or paprika (if using). Keep warm until ready to serve, stirring occasionally.

3. Assemble the Eggs Benedict:

- Place the toasted English muffin halves on serving plates.
- Top each half with a slice of Canadian bacon or cooked ham.
- Carefully place a poached egg on top of each muffin half.
- Spoon hollandaise sauce generously over each poached egg.

- Garnish with chopped chives or parsley if desired.

Serve Eggs Benedict immediately while warm. It pairs well with a side of roasted potatoes or fresh fruit. Enjoy this indulgent breakfast treat!

Breakfast burrito

Ingredients:

- 4 large eggs
- Salt and pepper, to taste
- 1 tablespoon butter or cooking oil
- 4 large flour tortillas (burrito size)
- 1 cup cooked breakfast sausage or bacon, chopped
- 1 cup shredded cheddar cheese
- 1/2 cup salsa or pico de gallo (optional)
- Chopped fresh cilantro or green onions (optional)
- Sour cream or avocado slices (optional)

Instructions:

1. **Prepare the Eggs:**
    - In a bowl, whisk together the eggs, salt, and pepper until well combined.
    - Heat a non-stick skillet over medium heat and add butter or oil.
    - Pour in the beaten eggs and cook, stirring gently, until the eggs are scrambled and cooked through. Remove from heat.
2. **Assemble the Breakfast Burritos:**
    - Lay out the flour tortillas on a clean surface.
    - Divide the scrambled eggs, cooked breakfast sausage or bacon, shredded cheese, and salsa (if using) evenly among the tortillas, placing the fillings in a line down the center of each tortilla.
3. **Roll the Burritos:**
    - Fold the sides of the tortillas over the filling.
    - Starting from the bottom edge closest to you, tightly roll the tortilla away from you, tucking in the sides as you go, to form a burrito shape.
4. **Serve or Wrap for Later:**
    - If serving immediately, you can optionally warm the assembled burritos in a skillet over medium heat for a few minutes on each side to crisp up the tortilla and melt the cheese.
    - If wrapping for later, you can wrap each burrito in foil or parchment paper to keep them warm and make them portable.
5. **Optional Garnishes:**
    - Serve the breakfast burritos with additional salsa or pico de gallo, chopped cilantro or green onions, sour cream, or avocado slices on the side.

Enjoy your homemade breakfast burritos as a delicious and filling start to your day!

Breakfast sandwich

Ingredients:

- 2 slices of bread (such as English muffins, sandwich bread, or bagels)
- 2 large eggs
- Salt and pepper, to taste
- 2 slices of cheese (cheddar, American, Swiss, or your favorite cheese)
- 2 slices of cooked bacon or breakfast sausage patties (optional)
- Butter or cooking oil for frying eggs

Instructions:

1. **Cook the Eggs:**
    - Heat a non-stick skillet over medium heat and add a little butter or oil.
    - Crack the eggs into the skillet and season with salt and pepper.
    - Cook the eggs to your preference (fried, scrambled, or as an omelette).
2. **Assemble the Sandwich:**
    - Toast the bread slices (if desired).
    - Place a slice of cheese on each bread slice to melt slightly.
    - Add the cooked eggs on one slice of bread.
    - If using, add cooked bacon or breakfast sausage on top of the eggs.
    - Top with the other slice of bread with the melted cheese.
3. **Serve:**
    - Cut the sandwich in half if desired and serve immediately while warm and melty.

You can customize your breakfast sandwich with additional toppings like avocado slices, tomatoes, spinach, or your favorite sauces such as ketchup, hot sauce, or mayo. Enjoy your homemade breakfast sandwich for a satisfying morning meal!

Bagels with cream cheese

Ingredients:

- Bagels (plain, sesame, everything, or your favorite variety)
- Cream cheese (plain or flavored, such as chive or strawberry)
- Optional toppings: Sliced tomatoes, cucumber, red onion, smoked salmon, capers, lettuce, etc.

Instructions:

1. **Prepare the Bagels:**
    - If the bagels are not pre-sliced, carefully slice them in half horizontally using a bread knife.
2. **Toast the Bagels (Optional):**
    - Toast the bagel halves in a toaster or toaster oven until they are golden brown and crispy (if you prefer toasted bagels).
3. **Spread Cream Cheese:**
    - Spread a generous amount of cream cheese on each toasted bagel half. Adjust the amount to your preference.
4. **Add Toppings (Optional):**
    - If desired, layer on additional toppings such as sliced tomatoes, cucumber, red onion, smoked salmon, capers, or lettuce.
5. **Assemble and Serve:**
    - Sandwich the bagel halves together with the cream cheese and toppings.
    - Serve immediately and enjoy your delicious bagels with cream cheese!

Bagels with cream cheese are versatile and can be enjoyed for breakfast, brunch, or as a snack any time of day. Feel free to customize your bagels with your favorite ingredients to suit your taste preferences.

Breakfast potatoes

Ingredients:

- 4 medium potatoes (russet or Yukon gold), peeled or unpeeled, diced into 1/2-inch cubes
- 2 tablespoons olive oil or melted butter
- 1 teaspoon paprika
- 1/2 teaspoon garlic powder
- 1/2 teaspoon onion powder
- 1/2 teaspoon dried thyme (optional)
- Salt and pepper, to taste
- Fresh parsley or chives, chopped (optional, for garnish)

Instructions:

1. **Preheat Oven:**
    - Preheat your oven to 400°F (200°C).
2. **Prepare Potatoes:**
    - Place the diced potatoes in a large bowl. Drizzle with olive oil or melted butter.
3. **Season Potatoes:**
    - Sprinkle paprika, garlic powder, onion powder, dried thyme (if using), salt, and pepper over the potatoes. Toss well to coat evenly.
4. **Bake Potatoes:**
    - Spread the seasoned potatoes in a single layer on a baking sheet lined with parchment paper or aluminum foil.
5. **Bake in Oven:**
    - Bake the potatoes in the preheated oven for about 25-30 minutes, or until they are crispy and golden brown. Stir the potatoes halfway through baking to ensure even cooking.
6. **Serve:**
    - Remove the potatoes from the oven and transfer them to a serving dish. Garnish with chopped fresh parsley or chives if desired.

Enjoy your homemade breakfast potatoes as a delicious side dish with eggs, breakfast meats, or as part of a breakfast burrito or sandwich. They're perfect for adding a crispy and flavorful touch to your morning meal!

Hash browns

Ingredients:

- 2 large russet potatoes, peeled (optional) and grated
- 2 tablespoons unsalted butter, melted (or vegetable oil)
- Salt and pepper, to taste
- Optional: chopped onion, bell peppers, or seasonings of your choice (such as paprika or garlic powder)

Instructions:

1. **Prepare the Potatoes:**
   - If desired, peel the potatoes. Use a box grater or a food processor with a grating attachment to grate the potatoes. Alternatively, you can finely dice them.
2. **Remove Excess Moisture (Optional):**
   - Place the grated potatoes in a clean kitchen towel or paper towels. Squeeze out as much moisture as possible from the potatoes. This helps in achieving crispy hash browns.
3. **Season the Potatoes:**
   - In a large bowl, toss the grated potatoes with melted butter (or oil), salt, pepper, and any optional seasonings or vegetables you'd like to add.
4. **Cook the Hash Browns:**
   - Heat a large non-stick skillet or cast iron skillet over medium heat. Add a little more butter or oil if needed.
   - Spread the seasoned potatoes evenly in the skillet, pressing them down with a spatula to form a compact layer.
   - Cook the hash browns for about 5-7 minutes on each side, or until they are golden brown and crispy. Use a spatula to carefully flip them halfway through cooking.
5. **Serve:**
   - Once both sides are crispy and golden brown, transfer the hash browns to a plate lined with paper towels to drain any excess oil.
   - Serve hot as a delicious side dish for breakfast, topped with ketchup, hot sauce, or alongside eggs and bacon.

Enjoy your homemade crispy hash browns for a satisfying breakfast! Adjust the seasoning and toppings according to your preferences for a personalized touch.

Breakfast sausage

Ingredients:

- 1 pound ground pork (you can also use ground turkey or chicken for a lighter option)
- 1 teaspoon salt
- 1/2 teaspoon ground black pepper
- 1/2 teaspoon dried sage
- 1/2 teaspoon dried thyme
- 1/4 teaspoon dried rosemary
- 1/4 teaspoon dried marjoram
- 1/4 teaspoon crushed red pepper flakes (optional, for a bit of heat)
- 1/4 teaspoon garlic powder
- 1/4 teaspoon onion powder
- Pinch of ground nutmeg (optional)
- 1-2 tablespoons olive oil or cooking oil, for frying

Instructions:

1. **Mix the Seasonings:**
    - In a small bowl, combine the salt, black pepper, sage, thyme, rosemary, marjoram, red pepper flakes (if using), garlic powder, onion powder, and nutmeg (if using). Mix well to evenly distribute the spices.
2. **Prepare the Sausage Mixture:**
    - In a large bowl, add the ground pork.
    - Sprinkle the mixed seasonings over the ground pork.
    - Use your hands to gently mix the seasonings into the ground pork until evenly combined. Be careful not to overmix.
3. **Form the Patties:**
    - Divide the sausage mixture into equal portions and shape them into patties about 1/2-inch thick. You can make them round or oval-shaped, depending on your preference.
4. **Cook the Sausage Patties:**
    - Heat a large skillet over medium heat and add olive oil or cooking oil.
    - Once the skillet is hot, add the sausage patties in a single layer, making sure not to overcrowd the pan.
    - Cook the patties for about 4-5 minutes per side, or until they are browned and cooked through. The internal temperature should reach 160°F (71°C) for pork or 165°F (74°C) for poultry.
5. **Serve:**
    - Once cooked, transfer the sausage patties to a plate lined with paper towels to drain any excess oil.
    - Serve hot alongside your favorite breakfast dishes, such as eggs, toast, or pancakes.

Enjoy your homemade breakfast sausage patties as a delicious and savory addition to your breakfast spread!

Bacon

Ingredients:

- Bacon slices (as many as you'd like)

Instructions:

1. **Pan-Frying Method:**
   - Heat a skillet or frying pan over medium heat.
   - Place the bacon slices in the skillet in a single layer, making sure they don't overlap.
   - Cook the bacon for about 4-5 minutes on each side, or until it reaches your desired level of crispiness. Use tongs to flip the bacon slices halfway through cooking.
   - Transfer the cooked bacon to a plate lined with paper towels to drain excess grease.
2. **Oven Method:**
   - Preheat your oven to 400°F (200°C).
   - Arrange the bacon slices in a single layer on a baking sheet lined with aluminum foil or parchment paper.
   - Bake the bacon in the preheated oven for about 15-20 minutes, or until it reaches your desired level of crispiness.
   - Remove the baking sheet from the oven and transfer the bacon slices to a plate lined with paper towels to drain excess grease.
3. **Microwave Method:**
   - Place a few layers of paper towels on a microwave-safe plate.
   - Lay the bacon slices on top of the paper towels in a single layer, making sure they don't overlap.
   - Cover the bacon with another layer of paper towels.
   - Microwave the bacon on high for about 1-2 minutes per slice, or until it reaches your desired level of crispiness.
   - Carefully remove the plate from the microwave (it will be hot) and transfer the bacon slices to a clean plate to cool slightly and drain excess grease.

Once cooked, enjoy your crispy bacon alongside eggs, pancakes, in sandwiches, or any way you like! Adjust the cooking time based on your preferred level of crispiness and the thickness of the bacon slices.

Biscuits and gravy

Ingredients:

For the Biscuits:

- 2 cups all-purpose flour
- 1 tablespoon baking powder
- 1/2 teaspoon baking soda
- 1 teaspoon salt
- 1/2 cup unsalted butter, cold and cut into small cubes
- 3/4 cup buttermilk (or regular milk)

For the Sausage Gravy:

- 1/2 pound breakfast sausage (pork or turkey)
- 1/4 cup all-purpose flour
- 2 cups milk
- Salt and pepper, to taste
- Optional: dash of cayenne pepper or paprika for a bit of heat

Instructions:

1. Make the Biscuits:

1. Preheat your oven to 450°F (230°C). Line a baking sheet with parchment paper or grease it lightly.
2. In a large bowl, whisk together the flour, baking powder, baking soda, and salt.
3. Add the cold cubed butter to the flour mixture. Use a pastry cutter or your fingertips to work the butter into the flour until the mixture resembles coarse crumbs.
4. Make a well in the center of the mixture and pour in the buttermilk. Use a fork or your hands to gently mix until the dough just comes together. Do not overmix.
5. Turn the dough out onto a lightly floured surface. Pat the dough into a rectangle about 1 inch thick.
6. Use a biscuit cutter or a glass to cut out biscuits. Place the biscuits on the prepared baking sheet, leaving a little space between each biscuit.
7. Bake the biscuits in the preheated oven for 10-12 minutes, or until they are golden brown on top. Remove from the oven and set aside while you prepare the gravy.

2. Make the Sausage Gravy:

1. In a large skillet or frying pan, cook the breakfast sausage over medium heat. Break up the sausage into small pieces as it cooks until it is browned and cooked through.
2. Sprinkle the flour over the cooked sausage. Stir well to coat the sausage with the flour, and cook for 1-2 minutes to cook out the raw flour taste.

3. Gradually pour in the milk, stirring constantly to avoid lumps. Bring the mixture to a simmer, stirring frequently.
4. Continue to cook and stir until the gravy thickens to your desired consistency, about 5-7 minutes. Season with salt, pepper, and cayenne pepper or paprika (if using), adjusting to taste.

3. Serve Biscuits and Gravy:

1. Split the warm biscuits in half and place them on serving plates.
2. Spoon the hot sausage gravy generously over the biscuits.
3. Serve immediately and enjoy your delicious homemade biscuits and gravy!

Biscuits and gravy are comforting and filling, perfect for a hearty breakfast or brunch. Adjust the seasoning and thickness of the gravy according to your preference.

Corned beef hash

Ingredients:

- 2 cups cooked corned beef, diced (leftover from a cooked corned beef brisket works great)
- 2 cups potatoes, peeled and diced into small cubes
- 1 small onion, finely chopped
- 2 tablespoons butter or cooking oil
- Salt and pepper, to taste
- Optional: chopped fresh parsley or green onions for garnish

Instructions:

1. **Prepare Potatoes:**
   - If using raw potatoes, place the diced potatoes in a saucepan and cover with water. Bring to a boil, then reduce heat and simmer for about 5 minutes until slightly tender. Drain and set aside.
2. **Cook Corned Beef Hash:**
   - In a large skillet or frying pan, melt the butter or heat the cooking oil over medium heat.
   - Add the chopped onions and cook until they become translucent and start to soften, about 3-4 minutes.
   - Add the diced potatoes to the skillet, spreading them out in an even layer. Allow them to cook without stirring too much, allowing them to brown and become crispy on one side, about 5-7 minutes.
   - Stir the potatoes and onions occasionally to ensure even cooking and browning.
3. **Add Corned Beef:**
   - Add the diced corned beef to the skillet, mixing it with the potatoes and onions.
   - Continue cooking for another 5-7 minutes, stirring occasionally, until the corned beef is heated through and the potatoes are crispy and golden brown.
4. **Season and Serve:**
   - Season the corned beef hash with salt and pepper to taste.
   - Optionally, garnish with chopped fresh parsley or green onions for added flavor and color.
   - Serve hot, either as a main dish or alongside eggs for a complete breakfast.

Enjoy your homemade corned beef hash, a comforting and delicious dish that makes great use of leftover corned beef! Adjust the seasoning and ingredients according to your taste preferences.

Cinnamon rolls

Ingredients:

For the dough:

- 4 cups all-purpose flour
- 1/3 cup granulated sugar
- 1 teaspoon salt
- 2 1/4 teaspoons (1 packet) instant yeast
- 1 cup milk, warmed to about 110°F (45°C)
- 6 tablespoons unsalted butter, melted and cooled
- 2 large eggs, at room temperature

For the filling:

- 1 cup packed light brown sugar
- 2 1/2 tablespoons ground cinnamon
- 6 tablespoons unsalted butter, softened

For the cream cheese icing:

- 4 ounces cream cheese, softened
- 1/4 cup unsalted butter, softened
- 1 cup powdered sugar
- 1/2 teaspoon vanilla extract
- Pinch of salt

Instructions:

1. Make the dough:

1. In a large mixing bowl, whisk together 3 1/2 cups of flour, sugar, salt, and yeast.
2. In a separate bowl, combine warm milk, melted butter, and eggs.
3. Pour the wet ingredients into the dry ingredients and stir until a soft dough forms.
4. Gradually add the remaining 1/2 cup of flour, a little at a time, until the dough is smooth and slightly sticky.
5. Transfer the dough to a lightly greased bowl, cover with plastic wrap or a clean kitchen towel, and let it rise in a warm place until doubled in size, about 1-2 hours.

2. Prepare the filling:

1. In a small bowl, mix together brown sugar and cinnamon.
2. Punch down the risen dough and transfer it to a lightly floured surface.
3. Roll out the dough into a rectangle, about 16x12 inches in size.
4. Spread softened butter evenly over the dough, leaving a small border around the edges.

5. Sprinkle the cinnamon sugar mixture evenly over the buttered dough.

3. Roll and cut the cinnamon rolls:

1. Starting from one long edge, tightly roll up the dough into a log.
2. Cut the log into 12 equal slices using a sharp knife or dental floss.
3. Place the cinnamon rolls in a greased 9x13 inch baking dish, leaving a little space between each roll.
4. Cover the rolls loosely with plastic wrap or a kitchen towel and let them rise in a warm place until they are puffy and have doubled in size, about 1 hour.

4. Bake the cinnamon rolls:

1. Preheat your oven to 350°F (175°C).
2. Remove the plastic wrap or towel from the risen rolls and bake them in the preheated oven for 25-30 minutes, or until they are golden brown on top.
3. Remove the cinnamon rolls from the oven and let them cool slightly in the pan on a wire rack while you prepare the icing.

5. Make the cream cheese icing:

1. In a medium bowl, beat together softened cream cheese and butter until smooth and creamy.
2. Add powdered sugar, vanilla extract, and a pinch of salt. Beat until smooth and well combined.
3. Spread the cream cheese icing evenly over the warm cinnamon rolls.

6. Serve and enjoy:

Serve the cinnamon rolls warm, allowing the icing to melt slightly over the rolls. Enjoy these homemade cinnamon rolls with a cup of coffee or tea for a delightful breakfast or anytime treat!

Quiche

Ingredients:

For the pastry crust:

- 1 1/4 cups all-purpose flour
- 1/2 teaspoon salt
- 1/2 cup cold unsalted butter, cut into small cubes
- 3-4 tablespoons ice water

For the quiche filling:

- 1 tablespoon olive oil or butter
- 1 small onion, finely chopped
- 1 cup chopped vegetables (spinach, bell peppers, mushrooms, broccoli, etc.)
- 1 cup grated cheese (such as Swiss, cheddar, or Gruyère)
- 4 large eggs
- 1 cup milk or heavy cream
- Salt and pepper, to taste
- Pinch of nutmeg (optional)

Instructions:

1. Make the pastry crust:

1. In a large bowl, whisk together the flour and salt.
2. Add the cold cubed butter to the flour mixture. Use a pastry cutter, fork, or your fingertips to cut the butter into the flour until the mixture resembles coarse crumbs.
3. Gradually add the ice water, 1 tablespoon at a time, mixing with a fork until the dough just comes together and forms a ball. Be careful not to overwork the dough.
4. Shape the dough into a disk, wrap it tightly in plastic wrap, and refrigerate for at least 30 minutes.
5. Preheat your oven to 375°F (190°C).
6. On a lightly floured surface, roll out the chilled dough into a circle about 12 inches in diameter. Carefully transfer the rolled-out dough to a 9-inch pie dish. Press the dough into the bottom and sides of the dish. Trim any excess dough and crimp the edges as desired. Prick the bottom of the crust with a fork.
7. Line the crust with parchment paper or aluminum foil and fill it with pie weights, dried beans, or rice.
8. Bake the crust in the preheated oven for 15 minutes. Remove the weights and parchment paper or foil, and bake for an additional 5 minutes, or until the crust is golden brown. Remove from the oven and set aside.

2. Prepare the quiche filling:

1. In a skillet, heat olive oil or butter over medium heat. Add the chopped onion and cook until softened and translucent, about 5 minutes.
2. Add the chopped vegetables to the skillet and cook until they are tender, about 5-7 minutes. Remove from heat and let cool slightly.
3. In a large bowl, whisk together the eggs and milk or cream until well combined. Season with salt, pepper, and a pinch of nutmeg if using.
4. Stir in the grated cheese and cooked vegetables into the egg mixture.

3. Assemble and bake the quiche:

1. Pour the egg and vegetable mixture into the pre-baked pastry crust.
2. Place the quiche on a baking sheet (to catch any spills) and bake in the preheated oven for 35-40 minutes, or until the filling is set and the top is golden brown.
3. Remove the quiche from the oven and let it cool for a few minutes before slicing and serving.
4. Serve warm or at room temperature. Quiche is delicious on its own or paired with a fresh salad for a complete meal.

Enjoy your homemade quiche, a versatile dish that can be customized with various ingredients to suit your taste preferences!

Breakfast pizza

Ingredients:

For the pizza dough:

- 1 pound (about 450g) pizza dough, homemade or store-bought
- Cornmeal or flour, for dusting

For the toppings:

- 1 cup shredded mozzarella cheese (or your favorite cheese blend)
- 4 large eggs
- 4 slices bacon, cooked and crumbled
- 4 breakfast sausage links, cooked and sliced
- 1/2 cup diced bell peppers
- 1/4 cup diced red onion
- Salt and pepper, to taste
- Chopped fresh parsley or chives, for garnish (optional)

Instructions:

1. **Preheat your oven:**
    - Preheat your oven to 475°F (245°C). If using a pizza stone, place it in the oven while preheating.
2. **Prepare the pizza dough:**
    - On a lightly floured surface, roll out the pizza dough to your desired thickness. Transfer the dough to a pizza peel or a parchment-lined baking sheet dusted with cornmeal or flour.
3. **Assemble the pizza:**
    - Sprinkle the shredded mozzarella cheese evenly over the pizza dough, leaving a small border around the edges for the crust.
    - Distribute the cooked and crumbled bacon, sliced breakfast sausage, diced bell peppers, and diced red onion over the cheese.
    - Create small wells or indentations in the toppings for cracking the eggs.
4. **Add the eggs:**
    - Crack each egg into a small bowl first (to prevent any shell from getting into the pizza) and then carefully pour each egg onto the pizza, spreading them out evenly.
5. **Season:**
    - Season the entire pizza with salt and pepper to taste.
6. **Bake the pizza:**
    - If using a pizza stone, carefully slide the pizza onto the preheated stone using the pizza peel (or place the parchment-lined baking sheet directly into the oven).

- Bake the pizza in the preheated oven for 10-12 minutes, or until the crust is golden brown, the cheese is melted and bubbly, and the eggs are cooked to your desired doneness (with the yolks still slightly runny is typical for breakfast pizza).

7. **Finish and serve:**
    - Remove the pizza from the oven and let it cool slightly. Sprinkle with chopped fresh parsley or chives for garnish, if desired.
8. **Slice and enjoy:**
    - Slice the breakfast pizza into wedges and serve immediately while warm.

Enjoy your homemade breakfast pizza as a delicious and satisfying meal to start your day! You can customize the toppings based on your favorite breakfast flavors and ingredients.

Breakfast tacos

Ingredients:

- 8 small flour or corn tortillas
- 6 large eggs
- 1/4 cup milk
- Salt and pepper, to taste
- 1 tablespoon butter or cooking oil
- 1 cup cooked breakfast sausage, crumbled or chopped (optional)
- 1 cup shredded cheddar or Monterey Jack cheese
- 1 avocado, sliced
- Salsa, for serving
- Chopped fresh cilantro, for garnish (optional)
- Lime wedges, for serving (optional)

Instructions:

1. **Prepare the Tortillas:**
   - Heat the tortillas in a dry skillet over medium heat for about 15-20 seconds on each side, until they are warmed and pliable. Stack them on a plate and cover with a clean kitchen towel to keep warm.
2. **Scramble the Eggs:**
   - In a bowl, whisk together the eggs, milk, salt, and pepper until well combined.
   - Heat the butter or oil in a non-stick skillet over medium heat. Pour in the egg mixture and cook, stirring occasionally with a spatula, until the eggs are scrambled and just set. Remove from heat.
3. **Assemble the Tacos:**
   - Divide the scrambled eggs evenly among the warmed tortillas.
   - Top each taco with cooked breakfast sausage (if using), shredded cheese, avocado slices, and salsa.
4. **Serve:**
   - Garnish the tacos with chopped cilantro, if desired, and serve with lime wedges on the side.
5. **Enjoy:**
   - Serve immediately while warm and enjoy your delicious homemade breakfast tacos!

Feel free to customize your breakfast tacos with additional toppings such as diced tomatoes, diced onions, sour cream, or hot sauce, based on your preferences. They are perfect for a quick and satisfying breakfast or brunch!

Granola with yogurt and fruit

Ingredients:

- 2 cups rolled oats
- 1/2 cup nuts or seeds (such as almonds, pecans, or sunflower seeds)
- 1/4 cup honey or maple syrup
- 2 tablespoons coconut oil or vegetable oil
- 1/2 teaspoon vanilla extract
- 1/2 teaspoon ground cinnamon
- 1/4 teaspoon salt
- 2 cups Greek yogurt (plain or flavored)
- Fresh fruit (such as berries, bananas, peaches, or any fruit of your choice)
- Optional toppings: additional honey or maple syrup, chia seeds, flax seeds, or coconut flakes

Instructions:

1. **Make the Granola:**
   - Preheat your oven to 325°F (160°C). Line a baking sheet with parchment paper or a silicone baking mat.
   - In a large bowl, combine the rolled oats, nuts or seeds, honey or maple syrup, coconut oil or vegetable oil, vanilla extract, ground cinnamon, and salt. Mix well until everything is evenly coated.
   - Spread the granola mixture evenly onto the prepared baking sheet.
   - Bake for 20-25 minutes, stirring halfway through, until the granola is golden brown and crisp. Keep an eye on it to prevent burning.
   - Remove from the oven and let the granola cool completely on the baking sheet. It will continue to crisp up as it cools.
2. **Assemble the Granola with Yogurt and Fruit:**
   - In serving bowls or glasses, layer Greek yogurt, a spoonful of granola, and fresh fruit slices or berries.
   - Repeat the layers until you've used up all the ingredients, ending with a layer of yogurt on top.
3. **Serve and Enjoy:**
   - Drizzle with additional honey or maple syrup if desired, and sprinkle with optional toppings like chia seeds, flax seeds, or coconut flakes.
   - Serve immediately and enjoy your homemade granola with yogurt and fruit as a nutritious and satisfying breakfast or snack!

This recipe is versatile, so feel free to adjust the ingredients and quantities based on your preferences. You can also prepare a larger batch of granola and store it in an airtight container for future use.

Muffins (various flavors)

1. Blueberry Muffins:

Ingredients:

- 1 1/2 cups all-purpose flour
- 3/4 cup granulated sugar
- 1/2 teaspoon salt
- 2 teaspoons baking powder
- 1/3 cup vegetable oil or melted butter
- 1 large egg
- 1/3 - 1/2 cup milk (start with 1/3 cup and add more if needed)
- 1 teaspoon vanilla extract
- 1 cup fresh or frozen blueberries (if using frozen, do not thaw)

Instructions:

1. Preheat your oven to 400°F (200°C). Line a muffin tin with paper liners or grease the muffin cups.
2. In a large bowl, whisk together the flour, sugar, salt, and baking powder.
3. In another bowl, whisk together the vegetable oil or melted butter, egg, milk, and vanilla extract until well combined.
4. Pour the wet ingredients into the dry ingredients and stir gently with a spatula or wooden spoon until just combined. Do not overmix; the batter should be lumpy.
5. Gently fold in the blueberries until evenly distributed.
6. Divide the batter evenly among the muffin cups, filling each about 2/3 full.
7. Bake for 18-20 minutes, or until the muffins are golden brown and a toothpick inserted into the center comes out clean.
8. Remove the muffins from the oven and let them cool in the pan for 5 minutes before transferring them to a wire rack to cool completely.

2. Chocolate Chip Muffins:

Ingredients:

- 1 3/4 cups all-purpose flour
- 1/2 cup granulated sugar
- 2 teaspoons baking powder
- 1/2 teaspoon baking soda
- 1/2 teaspoon salt
- 1 cup milk
- 1/3 cup vegetable oil or melted butter
- 1 large egg
- 1 teaspoon vanilla extract
- 3/4 cup chocolate chips (semi-sweet or milk chocolate)

Instructions:

1. Preheat your oven to 375°F (190°C). Line a muffin tin with paper liners or grease the muffin cups.
2. In a large bowl, whisk together the flour, sugar, baking powder, baking soda, and salt.
3. In another bowl, whisk together the milk, vegetable oil or melted butter, egg, and vanilla extract until well combined.
4. Pour the wet ingredients into the dry ingredients and stir gently with a spatula or wooden spoon until just combined. Do not overmix.
5. Gently fold in the chocolate chips until evenly distributed.
6. Divide the batter evenly among the muffin cups, filling each about 2/3 full.
7. Bake for 18-20 minutes, or until the muffins are lightly golden and a toothpick inserted into the center comes out clean.
8. Remove the muffins from the oven and let them cool in the pan for 5 minutes before transferring them to a wire rack to cool completely.

3. Banana Nut Muffins:

Ingredients:

- 1 1/2 cups all-purpose flour
- 1 teaspoon baking powder
- 1/2 teaspoon baking soda
- 1/2 teaspoon salt
- 1/2 teaspoon ground cinnamon
- 3 ripe bananas, mashed (about 1 1/2 cups)
- 1/2 cup granulated sugar
- 1/4 cup unsalted butter, melted
- 1 large egg
- 1 teaspoon vanilla extract
- 1/2 cup chopped walnuts or pecans (optional)

Instructions:

1. Preheat your oven to 375°F (190°C). Line a muffin tin with paper liners or grease the muffin cups.
2. In a large bowl, whisk together the flour, baking powder, baking soda, salt, and ground cinnamon.
3. In another bowl, combine the mashed bananas, sugar, melted butter, egg, and vanilla extract. Mix until well combined.
4. Pour the wet ingredients into the dry ingredients and stir gently with a spatula or wooden spoon until just combined. Do not overmix.
5. Gently fold in the chopped nuts, if using.
6. Divide the batter evenly among the muffin cups, filling each about 2/3 full.

7. Bake for 18-20 minutes, or until the muffins are golden brown and a toothpick inserted into the center comes out clean.
8. Remove the muffins from the oven and let them cool in the pan for 5 minutes before transferring them to a wire rack to cool completely.

These muffin recipes are versatile and can be easily adapted by adding other mix-ins or toppings such as berries, dried fruits, or different types of nuts. Enjoy these homemade muffins for breakfast, snacks, or any time of the day!

Doughnuts

Ingredients:

For the doughnuts:

- 1 cup whole milk, warmed to about 110°F (45°C)
- 1/4 cup granulated sugar
- 2 1/4 teaspoons (1 packet) active dry yeast
- 2 large eggs
- 6 tablespoons unsalted butter, melted and cooled
- 4 cups all-purpose flour, plus more for dusting
- 1/2 teaspoon salt
- Vegetable oil, for frying

For the glaze:

- 2 cups powdered sugar
- 1/4 cup milk or water
- 1 teaspoon vanilla extract

Instructions:

1. Prepare the Dough:

1. In a small bowl, combine the warm milk and sugar. Sprinkle the yeast over the mixture and let it sit for about 5-10 minutes, until foamy.
2. In a large bowl or the bowl of a stand mixer fitted with a dough hook, whisk together the yeast mixture, eggs, and melted butter.
3. Add the flour and salt to the bowl. Mix on low speed until a dough forms.
4. Increase the speed to medium and knead the dough for about 5-7 minutes, until smooth and elastic. If kneading by hand, transfer the dough to a floured surface and knead for about 10 minutes.
5. Place the dough in a greased bowl, cover with plastic wrap or a clean kitchen towel, and let it rise in a warm place until doubled in size, about 1-2 hours.

2. Shape and Fry the Doughnuts:

1. Once the dough has doubled in size, punch it down and turn it out onto a lightly floured surface.
2. Roll out the dough to about 1/2-inch thickness. Use a doughnut cutter or two round cutters (one larger for the outer circle and one smaller for the hole) to cut out doughnuts. Alternatively, you can use a drinking glass and a small biscuit cutter or bottle cap for the hole.
3. Place the cut doughnuts and doughnut holes on a lightly floured baking sheet, cover loosely with a kitchen towel, and let them rise again for about 30 minutes, until puffed.

4. Heat about 2-3 inches of vegetable oil in a large pot or Dutch oven until it reaches 350°F (175°C). Carefully place a few doughnuts into the hot oil, being careful not to overcrowd the pot.
5. Fry the doughnuts for about 1-2 minutes per side, until golden brown. Remove them with a slotted spoon and transfer to a wire rack lined with paper towels to drain and cool.

3. Glaze the Doughnuts:

1. In a medium bowl, whisk together the powdered sugar, milk or water, and vanilla extract until smooth and well combined.
2. Dip each cooled doughnut into the glaze, turning to coat both sides. Allow any excess glaze to drip off, then place the glazed doughnuts back onto the wire rack to set.
3. Optionally, you can sprinkle the glazed doughnuts with toppings like sprinkles, chopped nuts, or shredded coconut while the glaze is still wet.

4. Serve and Enjoy:

- Serve the homemade doughnuts fresh and enjoy them with a cup of coffee or tea!

These homemade doughnuts are best enjoyed the day they are made, while they are still fresh and fluffy. They can be stored in an airtight container at room temperature for up to 2 days, but they are at their peak right after frying and glazing. Enjoy your delicious homemade treats!

Fruit salad

Ingredients:

- 2 cups strawberries, hulled and quartered
- 1 cup blueberries
- 1 cup grapes, halved
- 2 kiwis, peeled and sliced
- 1 mango, peeled and diced
- 1 banana, sliced
- 1 orange, peeled and segmented
- 1 tablespoon honey (optional)
- Fresh mint leaves, for garnish (optional)

Instructions:

1. **Prepare the Fruit:**
   - Wash and prepare all the fruits as needed. Cut larger fruits into bite-sized pieces.
2. **Assemble the Fruit Salad:**
   - In a large mixing bowl, combine the strawberries, blueberries, grapes, kiwis, mango, banana, and orange segments.
3. **Optional:**
   - Drizzle honey over the fruit for a touch of sweetness, if desired. Gently toss to combine.
4. **Chill and Serve:**
   - Cover the fruit salad and refrigerate for at least 30 minutes to allow the flavors to meld.
5. **Garnish and Enjoy:**
   - Before serving, garnish with fresh mint leaves for a burst of color and added freshness.

Tips:

- **Variety:** Feel free to use any combination of your favorite fruits. Other great additions include pineapple, raspberries, blackberries, apples, or pears.
- **Dressing:** For a tangy dressing, you can squeeze fresh lemon or lime juice over the fruit instead of honey.
- **Storage:** Fruit salad is best enjoyed fresh but can be stored in an airtight container in the refrigerator for up to 2 days. Note that some fruits may become softer over time.

This fruit salad is not only delicious but also packed with vitamins, minerals, and antioxidants. It's perfect for breakfast, brunch, picnics, or as a healthy dessert option. Adjust the recipe to suit your taste and enjoy the vibrant flavors of fresh fruits!

Smoothies

Basic Smoothie Formula:

Ingredients:

- **Base Liquid:** 1 cup (choose one or a combination)
    - Water
    - Milk (dairy or plant-based like almond milk, soy milk, coconut milk)
    - Yogurt (plain or flavored, Greek yogurt adds creaminess and protein)
    - Fruit juice (orange juice, apple juice, etc.)
- **Fruits:** 1-2 cups (fresh or frozen)
    - Bananas
    - Berries (strawberries, blueberries, raspberries)
    - Mango
    - Pineapple
    - Peaches
    - Kiwi
    - Avocado (adds creaminess)
- **Vegetables:** Optional, 1/2 - 1 cup (spinach, kale, cucumber, carrots)
- **Protein:** Optional, 1 scoop of protein powder, or Greek yogurt
- **Sweetener:** Optional, to taste (honey, maple syrup, agave nectar)
- **Extras:** Optional, add-ins for extra flavor or nutrition
    - Nut butter (peanut butter, almond butter)
    - Chia seeds, flaxseeds
    - Oats
    - Coconut flakes
    - Vanilla extract
    - Cinnamon or nutmeg

Instructions:

1. **Blend:** Place all ingredients into a blender.
2. **Blend until smooth:** Start on low speed, gradually increasing to high, until smooth. If the smoothie is too thick, add more liquid. If it's too thin, add more fruit or ice.
3. **Serve:** Pour into glasses and enjoy immediately.

Recipe Ideas:

1. Berry Banana Smoothie:

- 1 cup milk (dairy or plant-based)
- 1 banana, peeled and sliced
- 1 cup mixed berries (strawberries, blueberries, raspberries)
- 1/2 cup Greek yogurt (optional for added creaminess and protein)
- 1 tablespoon honey (optional, for sweetness)

- Handful of spinach (optional, for added nutrients)

2. Tropical Green Smoothie:

- 1 cup coconut water
- 1/2 cup pineapple chunks (fresh or frozen)
- 1/2 cup mango chunks (fresh or frozen)
- 1 banana, peeled and sliced
- Handful of spinach or kale
- 1 tablespoon chia seeds or flaxseeds (optional, for extra fiber)

3. Chocolate Peanut Butter Banana Smoothie:

- 1 cup almond milk (or milk of choice)
- 1 banana, peeled and sliced
- 2 tablespoons peanut butter
- 1 tablespoon cocoa powder
- 1 tablespoon honey (optional, for sweetness)
- Handful of ice cubes

Tips:

- **Frozen Fruit:** Using frozen fruit helps make your smoothie cold and creamy without needing to add ice.
- **Prep Ahead:** You can pre-cut and freeze fruits and vegetables in portions for quick smoothie making.
- **Customize:** Adjust the ingredients to suit your taste preferences and dietary needs.

Smoothies are versatile, and you can experiment with different combinations of fruits, vegetables, liquids, and add-ins to create your favorite flavors. They make excellent breakfasts, snacks, or post-workout refreshments. Enjoy blending your own delicious and nutritious smoothies at home!

Crepes

Ingredients:

- 1 cup all-purpose flour
- 2 large eggs
- 1/2 cup milk
- 1/2 cup water
- 2 tablespoons unsalted butter, melted
- 1 tablespoon granulated sugar (for sweet crepes, optional)
- 1/4 teaspoon salt

Instructions:

1. **Prepare the Batter:**
   - In a large mixing bowl, whisk together the flour, sugar (if making sweet crepes), and salt.
2. **Add Wet Ingredients:**
   - Make a well in the center of the flour mixture and add the eggs. Whisk the eggs while gradually incorporating the flour mixture.
   - Slowly pour in the milk and water, whisking continuously to combine and create a smooth batter.
3. **Incorporate Butter:**
   - Pour in the melted butter and whisk until the batter is smooth and free of lumps.
4. **Rest the Batter:**
   - Let the batter rest for at least 30 minutes at room temperature. This resting period allows the flour to hydrate fully and results in more tender crepes.
5. **Cook the Crepes:**
   - Heat a non-stick skillet or crepe pan over medium heat. Lightly grease the pan with butter or oil.
   - Pour about 1/4 cup of batter into the center of the hot pan. Immediately lift the pan and swirl it to spread the batter evenly into a thin circle.
   - Cook the crepe for about 1-2 minutes, until the edges start to lift from the pan and the bottom is golden brown.
   - Flip the crepe using a spatula and cook for another 1 minute on the other side, until lightly browned. Adjust heat as needed to prevent burning.
6. **Repeat:**
   - Transfer the cooked crepe to a plate and cover loosely with foil to keep warm. Repeat the process with the remaining batter, greasing the pan lightly between each crepe.

To Serve Crepes:

- **Sweet Crepes:** Fill with Nutella, fresh berries, sliced bananas, whipped cream, or a sprinkle of powdered sugar.

- **Savory Crepes:** Fill with ham and cheese, spinach and mushrooms, scrambled eggs, or smoked salmon and cream cheese.
- **Fold or Roll:** Fold or roll the crepes with your desired fillings and toppings.

Tips:

- **Pan Size:** Use a pan that allows you to easily swirl and flip the crepe. A 10-inch skillet or crepe pan works well.
- **Consistency:** The batter should be thin enough to spread easily in the pan but not too runny. If necessary, adjust by adding a little more milk or water.
- **Make Ahead:** Cooked crepes can be stacked with parchment paper between each crepe, wrapped in plastic wrap, and refrigerated for up to 2 days or frozen for longer storage. Reheat gently in a skillet or microwave before filling and serving.

Enjoy your homemade crepes with your favorite toppings and fillings for a delightful breakfast, brunch, or dessert!

Breakfast casserole

Ingredients:

- 6 slices of bread (white, whole wheat, or sourdough), cubed
- 1 lb (450g) breakfast sausage or bacon, cooked and crumbled
- 1 cup shredded cheddar cheese (or cheese of your choice)
- 6 large eggs
- 1 1/2 cups milk
- 1/2 teaspoon salt
- 1/2 teaspoon black pepper
- 1/2 teaspoon mustard powder (optional)
- 1/4 teaspoon paprika (optional)
- 1/4 cup chopped green onions or chives (optional)

Instructions:

1. **Prepare the Casserole:**
    - Preheat your oven to 350°F (175°C). Grease a 9x13 inch baking dish.
    - Spread the cubed bread evenly in the baking dish. Top with cooked and crumbled breakfast sausage or bacon, and sprinkle with shredded cheese.
2. **Prepare the Egg Mixture:**
    - In a large bowl, whisk together the eggs, milk, salt, pepper, mustard powder (if using), and paprika (if using) until well combined.
3. **Assemble the Casserole:**
    - Pour the egg mixture evenly over the bread, sausage (or bacon), and cheese in the baking dish. Use a spatula to gently press down on the bread cubes to ensure they soak up the egg mixture.
4. **Add Optional Ingredients:**
    - Sprinkle chopped green onions or chives on top of the casserole for added flavor and color, if desired.
5. **Bake the Casserole:**
    - Cover the baking dish with foil and bake in the preheated oven for 30 minutes.
    - Remove the foil and continue baking for an additional 15-20 minutes, or until the casserole is set and the top is golden brown.
6. **Serve:**
    - Let the casserole cool for a few minutes before slicing and serving.

Variations:

- **Vegetarian Option:** Omit the meat and add sautéed vegetables such as bell peppers, onions, spinach, or mushrooms.
- **Cheese:** Experiment with different types of cheese like Monterey Jack, Swiss, or feta.
- **Bread:** Use croissants, biscuits, or hash browns instead of bread cubes for a different texture.

- **Make Ahead:** You can assemble the casserole the night before, cover it with plastic wrap or foil, and refrigerate overnight. In the morning, bake as directed, adding a few extra minutes to the baking time if needed.

This breakfast casserole is versatile and can be customized to suit your taste preferences. It's perfect for brunch gatherings, holidays, or any occasion when you want a satisfying and delicious breakfast option.

English muffins with jam

Ingredients:

- English muffins, split
- Butter (optional)
- Jam or preserves (flavor of your choice)

Instructions:

1. **Toast the English Muffins:**
   - Preheat your toaster or toaster oven. Split the English muffins in half horizontally.
   - Place the English muffin halves into the toaster and toast until they are golden brown and crisp on the edges.
2. **Spread Butter (Optional):**
   - If desired, spread a thin layer of butter on each toasted English muffin half while they are still warm. This adds a creamy texture and enhances the flavor.
3. **Add Jam:**
   - Spoon a generous amount of your favorite jam or preserves onto each English muffin half. You can use strawberry, raspberry, blueberry, apricot, or any flavor you prefer.
4. **Serve:**
   - Arrange the English muffin halves on a plate and serve immediately while they are still warm and the jam is slightly melted.

Tips:

- **Variations:** You can also add a layer of cream cheese before spreading the jam for extra richness and flavor.
- **Homemade Jam:** If you enjoy making your own jams or preserves, homemade versions can add a personal touch to this simple breakfast.
- **Accompaniments:** English muffins with jam pair well with a cup of tea or coffee for a cozy breakfast or afternoon snack.

This quick and easy recipe is perfect for busy mornings or whenever you crave a sweet and satisfying treat. Enjoy your English muffins with jam!

Breakfast quesadilla

Ingredients:

- 2 large flour tortillas (8-10 inches in diameter)
- 4 large eggs
- 1/2 cup shredded cheddar cheese (or cheese of your choice)
- 4 slices cooked bacon or breakfast sausage, chopped (optional)
- 1/4 cup chopped bell peppers (any color)
- 1/4 cup chopped onion
- Salt and pepper, to taste
- Salsa, sour cream, or guacamole, for serving (optional)

Instructions:

1. **Prepare the Eggs:**
   - In a bowl, whisk together the eggs with a pinch of salt and pepper.
   - Heat a non-stick skillet over medium heat. Add a drizzle of oil or a pat of butter.
   - Pour in the eggs and cook, stirring occasionally, until they are scrambled and fully cooked. Remove from heat and set aside.
2. **Assemble the Quesadilla:**
   - Lay one tortilla flat on a clean surface. Sprinkle half of the shredded cheese evenly over the tortilla.
   - Spread the scrambled eggs evenly over the cheese.
   - Add the chopped bacon or breakfast sausage (if using), chopped bell peppers, and chopped onion.
   - Sprinkle the remaining shredded cheese over the toppings.
   - Place the second tortilla on top to cover the filling, pressing down gently.
3. **Cook the Quesadilla:**
   - Heat a large non-stick skillet or griddle over medium heat. Carefully transfer the assembled quesadilla to the skillet.
   - Cook for about 3-4 minutes on each side, or until the tortilla is golden brown and the cheese is melted and gooey.
4. **Serve:**
   - Remove the quesadilla from the skillet and transfer it to a cutting board. Let it rest for a minute before slicing into wedges.
   - Serve hot with salsa, sour cream, or guacamole on the side, if desired.

Variations:

- **Vegetarian Option:** Skip the bacon or sausage and add more vegetables like spinach, mushrooms, or tomatoes.
- **Spicy Option:** Add a sprinkle of chili flakes or diced jalapeños for extra heat.
- **Make it Ahead:** You can prepare the scrambled eggs and chop the ingredients ahead of time for a quicker assembly in the morning.

This breakfast quesadilla is versatile and can be customized with your favorite ingredients. It's perfect for a hearty breakfast or brunch that's easy to make and full of flavor. Enjoy!

Scones

Ingredients:

- 2 cups all-purpose flour
- 1/4 cup granulated sugar
- 1 tablespoon baking powder
- 1/2 teaspoon salt
- 1/2 cup unsalted butter, cold and cut into small pieces
- 1/2 cup heavy cream (plus extra for brushing)
- 1 large egg
- 1 teaspoon vanilla extract
- Optional: 1/2 cup dried fruit (such as currants, raisins, or cranberries), chocolate chips, or nuts

Instructions:

1. **Preheat the Oven:**
   - Preheat your oven to 400°F (200°C). Line a baking sheet with parchment paper or a silicone baking mat.
2. **Mix Dry Ingredients:**
   - In a large bowl, whisk together the flour, sugar, baking powder, and salt until well combined.
3. **Cut in Butter:**
   - Add the cold butter pieces to the flour mixture. Using a pastry cutter or your fingertips, work the butter into the flour mixture until it resembles coarse crumbs. Some larger pea-sized pieces of butter are okay.
4. **Combine Wet Ingredients:**
   - In a separate bowl, whisk together the heavy cream, egg, and vanilla extract.
5. **Form Dough:**
   - Pour the wet ingredients into the dry ingredients, along with any optional dried fruit, chocolate chips, or nuts. Stir gently with a fork or spatula until the dough starts to come together.
6. **Knead the Dough:**
   - Transfer the dough onto a lightly floured surface. Gently knead the dough a few times until it forms a cohesive ball. Be careful not to overwork the dough.
7. **Shape the Scones:**
   - Pat the dough into a circle or rectangle that is about 1-inch thick. Use a sharp knife or a bench scraper to cut the dough into 8 wedges or squares.
8. **Bake the Scones:**
   - Place the shaped scones onto the prepared baking sheet, leaving some space between each scone. Brush the tops of the scones lightly with heavy cream.
   - Bake in the preheated oven for 15-18 minutes, or until the scones are golden brown on top and cooked through. They should sound hollow when tapped on the bottom.

9. **Cool and Serve:**
    - Remove the scones from the oven and transfer them to a wire rack to cool slightly before serving.

Optional Glaze:

- If desired, you can drizzle the cooled scones with a simple glaze made from powdered sugar and a little milk or lemon juice for added sweetness.

Tips:

- **Cold Ingredients:** Ensure your butter and cream are cold. Cold butter helps create a flaky texture in the scones.
- **Handling the Dough:** Handle the dough as little as possible to prevent the scones from becoming tough. The dough should be just combined enough to hold together.
- **Variations:** Customize your scones by adding different mix-ins such as dried fruit, chocolate chips, nuts, or citrus zest.

These homemade scones are best enjoyed fresh from the oven with a cup of tea or coffee. They are a delightful treat for breakfast, brunch, or any time you want a comforting baked good.

Huevos rancheros

Ingredients:

- 4 large eggs
- 4 corn or flour tortillas
- 1 cup refried beans (canned or homemade)
- 1 cup salsa (store-bought or homemade)
- 1 avocado, sliced
- Fresh cilantro, chopped (for garnish)
- Salt and pepper, to taste
- Optional toppings: diced tomatoes, sliced jalapeños, sour cream, shredded cheese

Instructions:

1. **Warm Tortillas:**
   - Heat the tortillas in a dry skillet over medium heat for about 1 minute on each side until they are warm and slightly toasted. Keep them warm wrapped in a clean kitchen towel or foil.
2. **Prepare Refried Beans:**
   - Heat the refried beans in a small saucepan over low heat until heated through. Stir occasionally to prevent sticking.
3. **Cook the Eggs:**
   - In the same skillet used for the tortillas, crack the eggs one at a time and cook them to your liking (fried or scrambled). Season with salt and pepper.
4. **Assemble Huevos Rancheros:**
   - Place a warm tortilla on each plate. Spread a generous spoonful of refried beans over each tortilla.
   - Top the beans with cooked eggs. Spoon salsa over the eggs.
   - Arrange avocado slices on the side of the plate or over the eggs.
5. **Garnish and Serve:**
   - Garnish with chopped cilantro and any optional toppings you prefer, such as diced tomatoes, sliced jalapeños, sour cream, or shredded cheese.
6. **Serve Immediately:**
   - Serve the Huevos Rancheros immediately while warm. Enjoy with hot sauce or additional salsa on the side, if desired.

Tips:

- **Homemade Salsa:** If making homemade salsa, you can blend together tomatoes, onions, cilantro, jalapeños, lime juice, and salt to taste.
- **Variations:** Customize your Huevos Rancheros by adding ingredients like chorizo, black beans, or grilled vegetables.
- **Make it Ahead:** You can prepare the components ahead of time (beans, salsa) and assemble the dish just before serving.

Huevos Rancheros is a flavorful and satisfying breakfast that combines savory flavors with a bit of heat from the salsa and richness from the eggs and avocado. It's a perfect dish to start your day with a taste of Mexico!

Grits

Ingredients:

- 1 cup stone-ground grits (not instant)
- 4 cups water or broth (chicken or vegetable)
- 1 teaspoon salt
- 2 tablespoons butter
- Optional toppings: shredded cheese, cooked bacon or sausage, sautéed vegetables, chopped green onions

Instructions:

1. **Prepare the Grits:**
    - In a heavy-bottomed saucepan, bring the water or broth to a boil over high heat.
    - Gradually whisk in the grits and reduce the heat to low.
2. **Cook the Grits:**
    - Stir in the salt and simmer the grits, uncovered, stirring occasionally to prevent sticking, for about 20-25 minutes or until they are thick and creamy. The grits should be tender with a smooth texture.
3. **Add Butter:**
    - Remove the saucepan from the heat and stir in the butter until it melts and is well incorporated into the grits.
4. **Serve:**
    - Serve the grits hot as a side dish or base for other ingredients.
5. **Optional Toppings:**
    - If desired, top the grits with shredded cheese, cooked bacon or sausage crumbles, sautéed vegetables like bell peppers or mushrooms, or chopped green onions.

Tips:

- **Consistency:** Adjust the consistency of the grits by adding more liquid if they become too thick during cooking. Remember that they will thicken slightly as they cool.
- **Stone-Ground Grits:** Stone-ground grits have a more textured and nutty flavor compared to instant grits. They require longer cooking but are well worth the effort.
- **Variations:** Grits are versatile and can be flavored with different ingredients such as garlic, herbs, or even spices like paprika or cayenne pepper for a savory twist.

Grits are a comforting and versatile dish that can be enjoyed for breakfast, brunch, or as a side dish for lunch or dinner. They pair well with a variety of toppings and are a staple in Southern cuisine.

Sausage gravy and biscuits

Ingredients:

- **For the Biscuits:**
    - 2 cups all-purpose flour
    - 1 tablespoon baking powder
    - 1/2 teaspoon baking soda
    - 1 teaspoon salt
    - 6 tablespoons unsalted butter, cold and cut into small cubes
    - 1 cup buttermilk (or substitute with 1 cup milk mixed with 1 tablespoon vinegar or lemon juice)
- **For the Sausage Gravy:**
    - 1/2 lb (225g) breakfast sausage (pork or turkey), casings removed if using links
    - 1/4 cup all-purpose flour
    - 2 cups milk (whole milk preferred)
    - Salt and pepper, to taste
    - Optional: pinch of cayenne pepper or paprika for a subtle kick

Instructions:

1. **Make the Biscuits:**
    - Preheat your oven to 450°F (230°C).
    - In a large mixing bowl, whisk together the flour, baking powder, baking soda, and salt.
    - Add the cold butter cubes to the flour mixture. Use your fingertips or a pastry cutter to cut the butter into the flour until the mixture resembles coarse crumbs.
    - Gradually add the buttermilk, stirring with a fork or spatula until the dough just comes together and forms a shaggy mass.
    - Turn the dough out onto a lightly floured surface. Pat or roll the dough to about 1-inch thickness. Use a biscuit cutter or a drinking glass to cut out rounds of dough.
    - Place the biscuits on a baking sheet lined with parchment paper, leaving a little space between each biscuit. Bake for 10-12 minutes, or until the biscuits are golden brown on top.
    - Remove from the oven and set aside while you make the sausage gravy.
2. **Make the Sausage Gravy:**
    - In a large skillet or frying pan, cook the breakfast sausage over medium-high heat, breaking it up into small pieces with a spatula or wooden spoon. Cook until browned and cooked through, about 5-7 minutes.
    - Sprinkle the flour over the cooked sausage and stir well to combine, ensuring the flour coats the sausage evenly.
    - Cook the flour and sausage mixture, stirring constantly, for about 1-2 minutes to cook off the raw flour taste.

- Gradually pour in the milk, stirring constantly to avoid lumps. Bring the mixture to a simmer.
- Reduce the heat to medium-low and continue to cook, stirring occasionally, until the gravy thickens to your desired consistency. This usually takes about 5-10 minutes.
- Season the gravy with salt, pepper, and optionally a pinch of cayenne pepper or paprika for added flavor.

3. **Serve:**
   - Split the warm biscuits in half and place them on serving plates.
   - Ladle the hot sausage gravy over the biscuits.
   - Serve immediately, garnished with freshly ground black pepper if desired.

Tips:

- **Make Ahead:** You can prepare the biscuits and sausage gravy ahead of time. Reheat the gravy gently on the stove, and warm the biscuits in the oven before serving.
- **Variations:** For a different twist, you can add chopped green onions or a dash of hot sauce to the sausage gravy.
- **Side Suggestions:** Serve with scrambled or fried eggs, hash browns, or fresh fruit for a complete breakfast.

Sausage gravy and biscuits are a comforting and hearty dish that is perfect for weekend brunches or special occasions. Enjoy the rich flavors and comforting warmth of this Southern classic!

Blueberry pancakes

Ingredients:

- 1 cup all-purpose flour
- 1 tablespoon granulated sugar
- 1 teaspoon baking powder
- 1/2 teaspoon baking soda
- 1/4 teaspoon salt
- 3/4 cup buttermilk (or 3/4 cup milk mixed with 1 tablespoon vinegar or lemon juice)
- 1 large egg
- 2 tablespoons unsalted butter, melted
- 1/2 teaspoon vanilla extract
- 1/2 cup fresh or frozen blueberries (if using frozen, do not thaw)

Instructions:

1. **Prepare Dry Ingredients:**
   - In a large bowl, whisk together the flour, sugar, baking powder, baking soda, and salt.
2. **Prepare Wet Ingredients:**
   - In another bowl, whisk together the buttermilk, egg, melted butter, and vanilla extract until well combined.
3. **Combine Wet and Dry Ingredients:**
   - Pour the wet ingredients into the dry ingredients and gently stir until just combined. Be careful not to overmix; a few lumps in the batter are okay.
4. **Add Blueberries:**
   - Gently fold the blueberries into the pancake batter. If using frozen blueberries, fold them in gently without thawing to prevent them from bleeding too much into the batter.
5. **Cook the Pancakes:**
   - Heat a non-stick skillet or griddle over medium heat. Lightly grease the surface with butter or cooking spray.
   - For each pancake, pour about 1/4 cup of batter onto the skillet. Use the back of a spoon or ladle to spread the batter into a circle.
   - Cook the pancakes for 2-3 minutes, or until bubbles form on the surface. Flip the pancakes and cook for another 1-2 minutes, or until golden brown and cooked through.
6. **Serve:**
   - Serve the pancakes warm with butter, maple syrup, additional blueberries, or whipped cream if desired.

Tips:

- **Buttermilk Substitute:** If you don't have buttermilk, you can make a substitute by adding 1 tablespoon of vinegar or lemon juice to 3/4 cup of milk. Let it sit for 5 minutes before using.
- **Keeping Pancakes Warm:** Keep cooked pancakes warm in a low oven (about 200°F or 95°C) while you finish cooking the rest.
- **Variations:** You can add other mix-ins such as chocolate chips, sliced bananas, or nuts to the batter along with or instead of blueberries.

Enjoy these fluffy blueberry pancakes for a delightful breakfast or brunch! They're sure to be a hit with everyone at the table.

Banana bread

Ingredients:

- 2 to 3 ripe bananas, mashed (about 1 cup)
- 1/2 cup unsalted butter, melted
- 1/2 cup granulated sugar
- 1/2 cup brown sugar, packed
- 2 large eggs, beaten
- 1 teaspoon vanilla extract
- 1 1/2 cups all-purpose flour
- 1 teaspoon baking soda
- 1/2 teaspoon baking powder
- 1/2 teaspoon salt
- 1/2 teaspoon ground cinnamon (optional)
- 1/2 cup chopped nuts (walnuts or pecans, optional)

Instructions:

1. **Preheat the Oven:**
   - Preheat your oven to 350°F (175°C). Grease a 9x5 inch loaf pan or line it with parchment paper.
2. **Prepare the Batter:**
   - In a large mixing bowl, mash the ripe bananas with a fork or potato masher until smooth.
   - Stir in the melted butter until well combined.
   - Add the granulated sugar, brown sugar, beaten eggs, and vanilla extract. Mix well.
3. **Combine Dry Ingredients:**
   - In a separate bowl, whisk together the flour, baking soda, baking powder, salt, and ground cinnamon (if using).
4. **Mix Batter:**
   - Gradually add the dry ingredients to the wet ingredients, mixing until just combined. Be careful not to overmix; a few lumps are okay.
5. **Add Nuts (Optional):**
   - If using chopped nuts, gently fold them into the batter.
6. **Bake the Banana Bread:**
   - Pour the batter into the prepared loaf pan, spreading it evenly.
   - Bake in the preheated oven for 60 to 75 minutes, or until a toothpick inserted into the center of the bread comes out clean or with a few moist crumbs.
7. **Cool and Serve:**
   - Allow the banana bread to cool in the pan for about 10 minutes, then transfer it to a wire rack to cool completely before slicing.

Tips:

- **Ripe Bananas:** Use ripe bananas with brown spots for the best flavor and sweetness.
- **Variations:** Add chocolate chips, dried fruit (like raisins or cranberries), or a swirl of Nutella to the batter for different flavor variations.
- **Storage:** Store leftover banana bread wrapped tightly in plastic wrap or in an airtight container at room temperature for up to 3 days, or refrigerate for up to a week.

This homemade banana bread is moist, flavorful, and perfect for any occasion. Enjoy it warm with a spread of butter or cream cheese for a delicious treat!

Frittata

Ingredients:

- 8 large eggs
- 1/4 cup milk or heavy cream
- Salt and pepper, to taste
- 1 tablespoon olive oil or butter
- 1 cup diced vegetables (such as bell peppers, onions, spinach, tomatoes, mushrooms)
- 1 cup diced cooked meat (such as ham, bacon, sausage, chicken)
- 1/2 cup shredded cheese (such as cheddar, mozzarella, feta)
- Fresh herbs, chopped (optional, for garnish)

Instructions:

1. **Preheat the Oven:**
   - Preheat your oven to 350°F (175°C).
2. **Prepare Ingredients:**
   - In a bowl, whisk together the eggs, milk or cream, salt, and pepper until well combined. Set aside.
   - Heat the olive oil or butter in an oven-safe skillet (preferably non-stick) over medium heat.
3. **Cook Vegetables and Meat:**
   - Add the diced vegetables to the skillet and cook until they are softened, about 5-7 minutes. If using cooked meat, add it to the skillet and heat through.
4. **Add Eggs:**
   - Pour the egg mixture evenly over the vegetables and meat in the skillet. Stir gently with a spatula to distribute the ingredients evenly.
5. **Cook the Frittata:**
   - Cook the frittata on the stovetop for 3-4 minutes, gently lifting the edges with a spatula to let the uncooked egg mixture flow underneath.
6. **Add Cheese (Optional):**
   - Sprinkle the shredded cheese evenly over the top of the frittata.
7. **Finish in the Oven:**
   - Transfer the skillet to the preheated oven. Bake the frittata for 10-15 minutes, or until the eggs are set and the top is lightly golden brown.
8. **Serve:**
   - Remove the frittata from the oven and let it cool for a few minutes. Sprinkle with chopped fresh herbs, if desired.
9. **Slice and Serve:**
   - Slice the frittata into wedges or squares. Serve warm or at room temperature.

Tips:

- **Variations:** Frittatas are incredibly versatile. You can use any combination of vegetables, meats, and cheeses based on your preferences or what you have on hand.
- **Make-Ahead:** Frittatas can be made ahead of time and stored in the refrigerator. They can be served cold, at room temperature, or reheated gently in the oven or microwave.
- **Gluten-Free:** This recipe is naturally gluten-free, but be mindful of ingredients you add for variations.

Frittatas are a great way to use up leftover vegetables and meats and are perfect for feeding a crowd or for meal prep. They are delicious served with a side salad or crusty bread. Enjoy experimenting with different flavor combinations!

Greek yogurt with honey and nuts

Ingredients:

- Greek yogurt (plain or flavored, about 1 cup)
- Honey, to taste
- Mixed nuts (such as almonds, walnuts, pecans), chopped
- Optional: Fresh berries or dried fruit for garnish

Instructions:

1. **Prepare the Yogurt:**
   - Spoon the Greek yogurt into a serving bowl or individual serving cups.
2. **Drizzle with Honey:**
   - Drizzle honey over the yogurt according to your preference for sweetness. Start with about 1-2 tablespoons and adjust to taste.
3. **Add Nuts:**
   - Sprinkle the chopped mixed nuts over the yogurt and honey. You can use a variety of nuts for different flavors and textures.
4. **Garnish (Optional):**
   - If desired, garnish with fresh berries or dried fruit for added sweetness and color.
5. **Serve:**
   - Serve immediately and enjoy as a nutritious breakfast, snack, or dessert.

Tips:

- **Yogurt Variations:** Greek yogurt comes in plain or flavored varieties. You can use plain Greek yogurt and adjust the sweetness with honey, or use a flavored Greek yogurt for added flavor.
- **Nuts:** Feel free to use your favorite nuts or seeds. Toasting the nuts lightly can enhance their flavor.
- **Additional Toppings:** Experiment with other toppings such as granola, coconut flakes, or a sprinkle of cinnamon for added flavor and texture.

This Greek yogurt with honey and nuts recipe is quick to assemble and provides a good balance of protein, healthy fats, and carbohydrates, making it a nutritious choice for any time of day. Enjoy its creamy texture and delightful combination of flavors!

Oatmeal with toppings

Ingredients:

- 1 cup old-fashioned oats (rolled oats)
- 2 cups water or milk (dairy milk, almond milk, soy milk, etc.)
- Pinch of salt
- Optional: Sweetener (such as honey, maple syrup, brown sugar)
- Optional: Vanilla extract or ground cinnamon for flavor

Topping Ideas:

- Fresh fruits: Sliced bananas, berries (strawberries, blueberries, raspberries), diced apples, peaches, or mangoes
- Dried fruits: Raisins, cranberries, chopped dates, apricots
- Nuts and seeds: Chopped almonds, walnuts, pecans, sunflower seeds, chia seeds, flaxseeds
- Nut butters: Peanut butter, almond butter, cashew butter
- Sweeteners: Honey, maple syrup, agave nectar
- Dairy or non-dairy yogurt
- Coconut flakes or shredded coconut
- Chocolate chips or cocoa nibs
- Granola or muesli

Instructions:

1. **Cook the Oatmeal:**
   - In a saucepan, bring the water or milk to a boil over medium-high heat.
   - Stir in the oats and a pinch of salt. Reduce the heat to medium-low and simmer, stirring occasionally, for about 5-7 minutes or until the oats are soft and the mixture has thickened.
2. **Sweeten and Flavor (Optional):**
   - Stir in a sweetener such as honey, maple syrup, or brown sugar, if desired. You can also add a splash of vanilla extract or a sprinkle of ground cinnamon for extra flavor.
3. **Serve with Toppings:**
   - Divide the cooked oatmeal into bowls.
   - Arrange your desired toppings over the oatmeal. Be creative and combine different flavors and textures!
4. **Enjoy:**
   - Serve the oatmeal warm and enjoy immediately.

Tips:

- **Texture:** Adjust the consistency of the oatmeal by adding more or less liquid according to your preference.

- **Make-Ahead:** Oatmeal can be made ahead of time and stored in the refrigerator. Simply reheat it on the stove or in the microwave, adding a splash of milk or water to loosen it up.
- **Variations:** Experiment with different combinations of toppings to keep your breakfast interesting and varied.

Oatmeal with toppings is not only delicious but also a great way to start your day with a healthy and filling meal. It provides complex carbohydrates, fiber, and protein, making it a nutritious choice for breakfast or any time of day.

Cinnamon toast

Ingredients:

- Slices of bread (white, whole wheat, or your choice)
- Butter, softened
- Granulated sugar
- Ground cinnamon

Instructions:

1. **Prepare the Cinnamon Sugar Mixture:**
   - In a small bowl, combine 1/4 cup of granulated sugar with 1-2 teaspoons of ground cinnamon (adjust to your taste preference). Mix well to combine.
2. **Toast the Bread:**
   - Toast the slices of bread in a toaster until they are golden brown and crisp.
3. **Spread Butter:**
   - While the toast is still warm, spread a generous amount of softened butter evenly over each slice of toast.
4. **Sprinkle Cinnamon Sugar:**
   - Sprinkle the cinnamon sugar mixture generously over the buttered toast. Make sure to cover the entire surface with the cinnamon sugar mixture.
5. **Serve:**
   - Cut the cinnamon toast slices diagonally or into squares. Serve warm and enjoy!

Tips:

- **Variations:** You can customize your cinnamon toast by adding a drizzle of honey or maple syrup over the butter before sprinkling with cinnamon sugar. You can also use flavored butter or spread, such as cinnamon butter or vanilla butter.
- **Oven Method:** If you prefer not to use a toaster, you can also make cinnamon toast in the oven. Preheat your oven to 350°F (175°C), place the bread slices on a baking sheet, and toast them for about 5-7 minutes until lightly browned. Remove from the oven, spread with butter, sprinkle with cinnamon sugar, and return to the oven for another 1-2 minutes until the sugar melts slightly.
- **Storage:** Cinnamon toast is best enjoyed fresh and warm. If you have leftovers, store them in an airtight container at room temperature for up to a day. Reheat briefly in the toaster oven or microwave before serving.

Cinnamon toast is a nostalgic and comforting treat that's quick to make and satisfies those craving something sweet with a hint of spice. It's a classic breakfast option that appeals to both kids and adults alike!

Breakfast sliders

Ingredients:

- 12 slider rolls or dinner rolls
- 6 large eggs
- 6 slices of bacon, cooked until crispy
- 6 slices of cheese (such as cheddar, American, or Swiss)
- Salt and pepper, to taste
- Butter, for brushing
- Optional toppings: sliced avocado, tomato, spinach, or arugula

Instructions:

1. **Prepare the Eggs:**
    - In a bowl, whisk the eggs with a pinch of salt and pepper. Scramble the eggs in a non-stick skillet over medium heat until they are cooked through. Remove from heat.
2. **Assemble the Sliders:**
    - Preheat your oven to 350°F (175°C).
    - Slice the slider rolls in half horizontally and place the bottom halves in a baking dish.
    - Layer the cooked scrambled eggs evenly over the bottom halves of the rolls.
    - Place a slice of cheese over the eggs on each roll.
    - Break each slice of crispy bacon in half and arrange the pieces over the cheese.
    - Add any optional toppings like sliced avocado, tomato, spinach, or arugula if desired.
    - Place the top halves of the rolls over the fillings to create sandwiches.
3. **Brush with Butter:**
    - Melt butter and brush it over the tops of the sliders for a golden crust.
4. **Bake:**
    - Cover the baking dish with foil and bake in the preheated oven for about 10-15 minutes, or until the cheese is melted and the sliders are heated through.
5. **Serve:**
    - Remove from the oven and carefully separate the sliders. Serve warm and enjoy!

Tips:

- **Variations:** You can customize these breakfast sliders by adding sausage patties or links, swapping out the bacon for ham or turkey, or using different types of cheese.
- **Make-Ahead:** Prepare the sliders ahead of time and store them in the refrigerator. Bake them in the oven when ready to serve for a quick and convenient breakfast.
- **Serving Suggestions:** Serve with a side of fresh fruit, hash browns, or a green salad to complete the meal.

These breakfast sliders are perfect for a weekend brunch with family or for a grab-and-go breakfast during the week. They're filling, flavorful, and can be easily adapted to suit your tastes. Enjoy the combination of eggs, bacon, cheese, and more in each delicious bite!

Belgian waffles

Ingredients:

- 2 cups all-purpose flour
- 1/4 cup granulated sugar
- 1 tablespoon baking powder
- 1/2 teaspoon salt
- 1 3/4 cups milk
- 2 large eggs
- 1/2 cup unsalted butter, melted
- 1 teaspoon vanilla extract

Instructions:

1. **Preheat the Waffle Iron:**
   - Preheat your Belgian waffle iron according to the manufacturer's instructions.
2. **Prepare Dry Ingredients:**
   - In a large bowl, whisk together the flour, sugar, baking powder, and salt.
3. **Combine Wet Ingredients:**
   - In another bowl, whisk together the milk, eggs, melted butter, and vanilla extract until well combined.
4. **Mix Batter:**
   - Pour the wet ingredients into the bowl with the dry ingredients. Stir gently until just combined. It's okay if there are a few lumps in the batter.
5. **Cook the Waffles:**
   - Lightly grease the preheated waffle iron with non-stick cooking spray or brush with melted butter.
   - Pour enough batter onto the hot waffle iron to cover the grid (amount will depend on the size of your waffle iron).
   - Close the lid and cook according to the manufacturer's instructions, typically about 3-5 minutes, or until the waffle is golden brown and crisp.
6. **Serve:**
   - Carefully remove the cooked waffle from the iron using tongs or a fork. Repeat with the remaining batter.
   - Serve the Belgian waffles warm, topped with your favorite toppings such as fresh berries, whipped cream, maple syrup, powdered sugar, or a drizzle of chocolate sauce.

Tips:

- **Waffle Iron:** Belgian waffle irons typically have deeper grids than regular waffle irons, allowing for thicker waffles with deeper pockets. Adjust the amount of batter according to your waffle iron size.

- **Variations:** You can customize your Belgian waffles by adding chocolate chips, chopped nuts, or cinnamon to the batter before cooking.
- **Make-Ahead:** If you have leftover waffles, let them cool completely and then store them in an airtight container in the refrigerator for up to 3 days. Reheat in a toaster or oven until warmed through.

Belgian waffles are a beloved breakfast option that can be enjoyed with a variety of toppings, making them a versatile and delicious choice for any morning meal or brunch.

Breakfast wraps

Ingredients:

- Large flour tortillas (8 or 10-inch size)
- Eggs (2-3 per wrap, depending on size)
- Salt and pepper, to taste
- Cooking oil or butter
- Fillings (choose from options below):
    - Cooked breakfast meats (such as bacon, sausage, ham)
    - Vegetables (such as bell peppers, onions, spinach, tomatoes)
    - Cheese (shredded cheddar, mozzarella, feta)
    - Avocado slices or guacamole
    - Salsa or hot sauce
    - Fresh herbs (such as cilantro or parsley)

Instructions:

1. **Prepare Fillings:**
    - Cook any meats (like bacon or sausage) until crispy or fully cooked. Set aside.
    - Saute vegetables in a pan until tender. Set aside.
    - Whisk eggs in a bowl with salt and pepper.
2. **Cook Eggs:**
    - Heat a non-stick skillet over medium heat. Add a little oil or butter to coat the pan.
    - Pour in the whisked eggs and cook, stirring occasionally, until they are scrambled and fully cooked. Remove from heat.
3. **Assemble Wraps:**
    - Lay a tortilla flat on a clean surface.
    - Spread a layer of scrambled eggs across the center of the tortilla.
    - Add your desired fillings on top of the eggs, such as cooked meats, sautéed vegetables, cheese, avocado slices, salsa, and herbs.
4. **Wrap It Up:**
    - Fold in the sides of the tortilla over the filling.
    - Roll up the tortilla tightly from bottom to top to form a wrap.
5. **Serve:**
    - Serve the breakfast wraps immediately, or wrap them in foil for an on-the-go meal.

Tips:

- **Variations:** Customize your breakfast wraps with different combinations of fillings. You can make them vegetarian by omitting meat and adding more veggies. Experiment with different cheeses and sauces for added flavor.

- **Make-Ahead:** Breakfast wraps can be prepared ahead of time and stored in the refrigerator. To reheat, wrap them in foil and warm them in the oven or microwave until heated through.
- **Serving Suggestions:** Serve breakfast wraps with fresh fruit, hash browns, or a side of yogurt for a complete meal.

Breakfast wraps are versatile and can be adapted to suit your taste preferences. They're perfect for busy mornings when you want a quick and satisfying breakfast option that you can take with you wherever you go. Enjoy experimenting with different ingredients to create your favorite breakfast wrap!

Breakfast strata

Ingredients:

- 8 cups cubed bread (such as French bread, ciabatta, or sourdough)
- 1 cup cooked and crumbled breakfast sausage, bacon, or ham (optional)
- 1 cup shredded cheese (such as cheddar, mozzarella, Swiss, or a combination)
- 1 cup vegetables (such as spinach, bell peppers, mushrooms, onions), sautéed and drained if necessary
- 8 large eggs
- 2 cups milk (whole milk or half-and-half)
- 1 teaspoon Dijon mustard (optional)
- 1/2 teaspoon salt
- 1/4 teaspoon black pepper
- Fresh herbs (such as parsley or chives), chopped, for garnish

Instructions:

1. **Prepare the Bread and Layering:**
    - Grease a 9x13 inch baking dish with butter or cooking spray. Spread half of the cubed bread in the bottom of the dish.
    - Layer half of the cooked sausage, bacon, or ham (if using), half of the shredded cheese, and half of the sautéed vegetables over the bread cubes.
    - Repeat with another layer of bread cubes, sausage (if using), cheese, and vegetables.
2. **Prepare the Egg Mixture:**
    - In a large bowl, whisk together the eggs, milk, Dijon mustard (if using), salt, and black pepper until well combined.
3. **Pour and Refrigerate:**
    - Pour the egg mixture evenly over the layered ingredients in the baking dish. Use a spatula to gently press down on the bread cubes to help them absorb the liquid.
    - Cover the baking dish with plastic wrap and refrigerate for at least 2 hours or overnight. This allows the bread to soak up the egg mixture.
4. **Bake the Strata:**
    - Preheat your oven to 350°F (175°C).
    - Remove the plastic wrap from the baking dish and bake the strata, uncovered, for 45-55 minutes, or until the top is golden brown and the eggs are set.
5. **Serve:**
    - Let the strata cool for a few minutes before slicing and serving. Garnish with chopped fresh herbs, if desired.

Tips:

- **Variations:** Feel free to customize your breakfast strata with different combinations of meats, cheeses, and vegetables. You can also add herbs like thyme or basil for additional flavor.
- **Make-Ahead:** Prepare the strata the night before, refrigerate overnight, and bake it in the morning for an easy and delicious breakfast or brunch.
- **Leftovers:** Leftover strata can be stored in an airtight container in the refrigerator for up to 3 days. Reheat individual servings in the microwave or oven.

Breakfast strata is a comforting and satisfying dish that's perfect for serving a crowd or for a special weekend breakfast. It's versatile, allowing you to use up leftover ingredients and customize it to your preferences. Enjoy this savory treat with your favorite brunch beverages!

Pancake skewers

Ingredients:

- Pancake batter (you can use your favorite pancake recipe or a pancake mix)
- Skewers (wooden or metal)

Optional Toppings:

- Fresh fruit (such as strawberries, bananas, blueberries)
- Miniature sausages or bacon pieces
- Maple syrup or honey, for drizzling
- Whipped cream
- Chocolate chips
- Nutella or other spreads
- Powdered sugar, for dusting

Instructions:

1. **Prepare Pancake Batter:**
   - Prepare your pancake batter according to the recipe or package instructions.
2. **Cook Pancakes:**
   - Heat a non-stick griddle or frying pan over medium heat. Lightly grease the surface with butter or cooking spray.
   - Pour small rounds of pancake batter onto the griddle, using about 1-2 tablespoons of batter per pancake (depending on the size of your skewers). Cook until bubbles form on the surface of the pancakes, then flip and cook until golden brown on both sides. Repeat until all batter is used.
3. **Cut Pancakes:**
   - Once the pancakes are cooked and cooled slightly, cut them into bite-sized squares or rectangles that are about 1-2 inches in size.
4. **Assemble Pancake Skewers:**
   - Thread the pancake squares onto skewers, alternating with your desired toppings such as fresh fruit, miniature sausages or bacon pieces, and chocolate chips.
5. **Serve:**
   - Arrange the pancake skewers on a serving platter.
   - Serve with maple syrup or honey for drizzling, whipped cream for dipping, and powdered sugar for dusting.

Tips:

- **Variations:** Get creative with your pancake skewers by adding different toppings and flavors. You can also use different shapes of pancakes (like mini pancakes or heart-shaped pancakes) for variety.
- **Make-Ahead:** You can prepare the pancakes and toppings ahead of time. Assemble the skewers just before serving to keep them fresh and appealing.

- **Kid-Friendly:** Pancake skewers are a hit with kids and can be a fun activity to involve them in the kitchen.

Pancake skewers are not only delicious but also visually appealing, making them a great choice for brunch parties or special breakfast occasions. They allow your guests to enjoy a variety of flavors and textures in each bite. Enjoy making and serving these delightful pancake skewers!

Breakfast BLT

Ingredients:

- 4 slices of thick-cut bacon
- 2 large eggs
- 4 slices of bread (toasted)
- Mayonnaise or aioli
- Lettuce leaves (romaine, green leaf, or your favorite)
- Sliced tomatoes
- Salt and pepper, to taste

Optional Additions:

- Avocado slices
- Sliced cheese (cheddar, Swiss, or your favorite)
- Hot sauce or Sriracha for added kick

Instructions:

1. **Cook the Bacon:**
    - In a skillet over medium heat, cook the bacon until crispy. Remove and drain on paper towels.
2. **Cook the Eggs:**
    - In the same skillet with the bacon drippings, fry the eggs to your desired doneness (fried or scrambled).
3. **Assemble the Sandwich:**
    - Spread mayonnaise or aioli on one side of each slice of toasted bread.
    - Layer lettuce leaves on one slice of bread.
    - Top with sliced tomatoes.
    - Add the cooked bacon slices.
    - Place the fried or scrambled eggs on top of the bacon.
    - Season with salt and pepper.
    - Optionally, add avocado slices, cheese slices, or a drizzle of hot sauce.
4. **Top and Serve:**
    - Place the second slice of bread on top to close the sandwich.
    - Cut the sandwich in half diagonally or serve whole.
    - Serve immediately while warm and enjoy your delicious Breakfast BLT!

Tips:

- **Bread Choice:** Choose your favorite type of bread for toasting, such as whole wheat, sourdough, or brioche, for added flavor.
- **Make-Ahead:** Cook the bacon and prepare the ingredients ahead of time for quicker assembly in the morning.
- **Variations:** Experiment with different toppings or spreads, such as guacamole or pesto, to customize your Breakfast BLT to your liking.

A Breakfast BLT is a satisfying and flavorful way to start your day, combining the classic flavors of bacon, lettuce, and tomato with eggs for added protein. It's perfect for a leisurely weekend breakfast or a quick weekday brunch. Enjoy this hearty sandwich with a side of fresh fruit or hash browns for a complete meal!

Breakfast pita

Ingredients:

- 2 large pita bread rounds (whole wheat or white)
- 4 large eggs
- 1/2 cup diced bell peppers (any color)
- 1/2 cup diced onions
- 1/2 cup diced tomatoes
- 1/2 cup cooked and crumbled breakfast sausage or bacon (optional)
- 1/2 cup shredded cheese (such as cheddar, mozzarella, or feta)
- Salt and pepper, to taste
- Cooking oil or butter

Optional Toppings:

- Fresh herbs (such as parsley or chives), chopped
- Salsa or hot sauce
- Avocado slices or guacamole

Instructions:

1. **Prepare the Fillings:**
    - In a skillet, heat a drizzle of oil or melt butter over medium heat.
    - Add diced bell peppers and onions to the skillet. Sauté for 3-4 minutes until softened.
    - Add diced tomatoes and cook for an additional 1-2 minutes until heated through. Season with salt and pepper to taste.
    - If using, add cooked and crumbled breakfast sausage or bacon to the skillet and heat through.
2. **Scramble the Eggs:**
    - In a bowl, whisk the eggs with a pinch of salt and pepper.
    - Pour the whisked eggs into the skillet with the vegetables and sausage. Cook over medium heat, stirring occasionally, until the eggs are scrambled and fully cooked.
3. **Assemble the Breakfast Pitas:**
    - Warm the pita bread rounds in a toaster or oven until slightly crisp.
    - Cut each pita bread in half to form pockets.
    - Spoon the scrambled egg mixture into each pita pocket.
    - Sprinkle shredded cheese over the eggs while they are still warm so it melts slightly.
4. **Serve:**
    - Garnish with chopped fresh herbs, if desired.
    - Add optional toppings such as salsa, hot sauce, or avocado slices.
    - Serve immediately and enjoy your delicious breakfast pita!

Tips:

- **Variations:** Customize your breakfast pita by adding different vegetables, cheeses, or meats. You can also omit the meat for a vegetarian option.
- **Make-Ahead:** Prepare the scrambled egg mixture ahead of time and store it in the refrigerator. Reheat gently before assembling the breakfast pitas.
- **Portable Option:** Wrap the assembled breakfast pitas in foil or parchment paper for an easy grab-and-go breakfast.

Breakfast pitas are versatile and can be enjoyed with various fillings and toppings, making them a satisfying and flavorful choice for any morning. They're perfect for a quick weekday breakfast or a leisurely weekend brunch. Enjoy experimenting with different combinations to create your favorite breakfast pita!

Chilaquiles

Ingredients:

- 1 tablespoon vegetable oil
- 1 small onion, finely chopped
- 2 cloves garlic, minced
- 1 jalapeño or serrano chili, seeded and finely chopped (optional, for heat)
- 2 cups tomato sauce or salsa (choose your preferred level of spiciness)
- 1 cup chicken or vegetable broth
- Salt and pepper, to taste
- 8-10 corn tortillas, cut into triangles or strips
- Vegetable oil, for frying tortillas
- 4-6 large eggs (1-2 eggs per serving)
- 1 cup shredded cheese (such as Monterey Jack or cheddar)
- Optional toppings: chopped fresh cilantro, sliced avocado, crumbled queso fresco or cotija cheese, sour cream or Mexican crema, sliced radishes

Instructions:

1. **Prepare the Sauce:**
   - In a large skillet or saucepan, heat 1 tablespoon of vegetable oil over medium heat.
   - Add the chopped onion and sauté until softened, about 3-4 minutes.
   - Stir in the minced garlic and chopped chili (if using), and cook for another minute until fragrant.
   - Add the tomato sauce or salsa and chicken broth. Season with salt and pepper to taste. Bring to a simmer and let it cook for about 10 minutes, stirring occasionally, until the sauce thickens slightly.
2. **Prepare the Tortillas:**
   - While the sauce is simmering, heat about 1/4 inch of vegetable oil in a separate skillet over medium-high heat.
   - Working in batches, fry the tortilla strips or triangles until crispy and golden brown, about 1-2 minutes per side. Use tongs to transfer the fried tortillas to a plate lined with paper towels to drain excess oil.
3. **Assemble the Chilaquiles:**
   - Once all the tortillas are fried, add them to the simmering sauce in the skillet. Gently stir to coat the tortillas evenly with the sauce.
   - Make small wells in the mixture and crack the eggs directly into the sauce. Cover the skillet with a lid and cook until the eggs are set to your liking, about 5-7 minutes for runny yolks or longer for firmer yolks.
4. **Serve:**
   - Sprinkle shredded cheese over the chilaquiles and cover the skillet again for a minute or two until the cheese melts.
   - Remove from heat and garnish with chopped fresh cilantro, sliced avocado, crumbled queso fresco or cotija cheese, and a dollop of sour cream or Mexican crema.

- Serve the chilaquiles immediately, directly from the skillet, with warm corn tortillas or crusty bread on the side.

Tips:

- **Variations:** Chilaquiles can be customized with different toppings and additions. You can add shredded chicken, beans, or extra vegetables to the sauce for added protein and flavor.
- **Serving Suggestions:** Serve chilaquiles as a standalone breakfast dish or as part of a larger Mexican-inspired brunch spread.
- **Make-Ahead:** The sauce and fried tortillas can be prepared ahead of time. Reheat the sauce and tortillas separately before assembling the dish with the eggs and toppings.

Chilaquiles are a comforting and flavorful breakfast option that combines crispy tortillas with a savory sauce and eggs. It's a dish that's sure to satisfy both your hunger and your taste buds!

Avocado toast with eggs

Ingredients:

- 2 slices of bread (whole wheat, sourdough, or your favorite)
- 1 ripe avocado
- 2-4 eggs (depending on how many you prefer)
- Salt and pepper, to taste
- Optional toppings: cherry tomatoes, microgreens, red pepper flakes, feta cheese, or a drizzle of balsamic glaze

Instructions:

1. **Prepare the Avocado:**
   - Cut the avocado in half lengthwise, remove the pit, and scoop the flesh into a bowl.
   - Mash the avocado with a fork until smooth or slightly chunky, depending on your preference.
   - Season the mashed avocado with salt and pepper to taste.
2. **Toast the Bread:**
   - Toast the slices of bread until golden brown and crisp.
3. **Cook the Eggs:**
   - While the bread is toasting, prepare the eggs. You can cook them sunny-side-up, over easy, scrambled, or poached—whichever way you prefer.
   - For sunny-side-up or over easy eggs, heat a non-stick skillet over medium heat. Add a little butter or cooking oil. Crack the eggs into the skillet and cook until the whites are set but the yolks are still runny.
   - For scrambled eggs, whisk the eggs in a bowl with a pinch of salt and pepper. Cook them in a skillet over medium heat, stirring gently until they are scrambled and cooked through.
4. **Assemble the Avocado Toast:**
   - Spread the mashed avocado evenly onto the toasted bread slices.
   - Top each slice with cooked eggs.
5. **Add Optional Toppings:**
   - Garnish the avocado toast with any optional toppings you prefer, such as sliced cherry tomatoes, microgreens, red pepper flakes, crumbled feta cheese, or a drizzle of balsamic glaze.
6. **Serve:**
   - Serve the avocado toast with eggs immediately, while warm.

Tips:

- **Variations:** Customize your avocado toast with different toppings and seasonings. You can add sliced radishes, cucumber, or smoked salmon for additional flavor and texture.
- **Make-Ahead:** Prepare the mashed avocado and toast the bread ahead of time. Cook the eggs just before assembling the avocado toast to ensure they are hot and fresh.
- **Nutritional Benefits:** Avocado toast with eggs is a balanced breakfast option, providing healthy fats from avocado, protein from eggs, and complex carbohydrates from whole grain bread.

Avocado toast with eggs is not only delicious but also quick and easy to make, making it perfect for busy mornings or leisurely brunches. Enjoy this wholesome dish as a satisfying start to your day!

Breakfast flatbread

Ingredients:

- 1 large flatbread or naan bread (store-bought or homemade)
- 2-3 large eggs

- 1/2 cup shredded cheese (such as mozzarella, cheddar, or a blend)
- 1/4 cup diced bell peppers (any color)
- 1/4 cup diced onions
- 1/4 cup diced tomatoes
- 2 slices of cooked bacon or sausage, crumbled (optional)
- Salt and pepper, to taste
- Fresh herbs (such as parsley or chives), chopped for garnish (optional)
- Olive oil or cooking spray

Instructions:

1. **Prepare the Flatbread:**
   - Preheat your oven to 400°F (200°C).
   - Place the flatbread on a baking sheet. If the flatbread is not pre-cooked, brush it lightly with olive oil and bake for 5-7 minutes until it starts to crisp up slightly. This step ensures the flatbread will hold up well with the toppings.
2. **Cook the Eggs:**
   - While the flatbread is pre-cooking, scramble or fry the eggs according to your preference in a non-stick skillet. Season with salt and pepper to taste.
3. **Assemble the Breakfast Flatbread:**
   - Remove the flatbread from the oven (if pre-cooked). Spread a thin layer of olive oil or cooking spray over the surface.
   - Evenly distribute the scrambled or fried eggs over the flatbread.
   - Sprinkle the shredded cheese over the eggs.
   - Scatter the diced bell peppers, onions, tomatoes, and crumbled bacon or sausage (if using) over the cheese.
4. **Bake the Flatbread:**
   - Place the assembled flatbread back into the oven and bake for another 8-10 minutes, or until the cheese is melted and bubbly.
5. **Serve:**
   - Remove the breakfast flatbread from the oven and let it cool slightly.
   - Sprinkle with chopped fresh herbs, if desired, for added flavor and freshness.
   - Cut the flatbread into slices or squares and serve immediately.

Tips:

- **Variations:** You can customize your breakfast flatbread with various toppings such as avocado slices, cooked spinach, mushrooms, or different types of cheese.
- **Make-Ahead:** Prep the toppings ahead of time for a quicker assembly in the morning. You can also prepare the flatbread up to the baking step and store it in the refrigerator until ready to bake.
- **Serving Suggestions:** Serve the breakfast flatbread with a side of fresh fruit or a simple salad for a complete meal.

This breakfast flatbread is a delicious and satisfying option that combines crispy flatbread with savory eggs, cheese, and vegetables. It's perfect for a weekend brunch or even a quick weekday breakfast. Enjoy experimenting with different flavors and toppings to create your favorite version!

Quinoa breakfast bowl

Ingredients:

- 1 cup quinoa
- 2 cups water or vegetable broth

- Pinch of salt
- 4 large eggs
- 1 avocado, sliced
- 1 cup cherry tomatoes, halved
- 1/2 cucumber, diced
- 1/4 cup red onion, finely chopped
- 1/4 cup fresh cilantro, chopped
- Juice of 1 lemon or lime
- Salt and pepper, to taste
- Optional toppings: crumbled feta cheese, toasted nuts or seeds, hot sauce

Instructions:

1. **Cook the Quinoa:**
    - Rinse the quinoa under cold water using a fine-mesh sieve.
    - In a medium saucepan, combine the quinoa, water or vegetable broth, and a pinch of salt. Bring to a boil over medium-high heat.
    - Reduce the heat to low, cover, and simmer for 15-20 minutes, or until the quinoa is cooked and the liquid is absorbed. Remove from heat and let it sit covered for 5 minutes. Fluff with a fork.
2. **Prepare the Eggs:**
    - While the quinoa is cooking, prepare the eggs to your liking. You can scramble, fry, or poach them.
3. **Assemble the Breakfast Bowl:**
    - Divide the cooked quinoa evenly among serving bowls.
    - Arrange the sliced avocado, cherry tomatoes, diced cucumber, and chopped red onion on top of the quinoa.
    - Place the cooked eggs on one side of the bowl.
4. **Season and Garnish:**
    - Drizzle the lemon or lime juice over the ingredients in each bowl.
    - Season with salt and pepper to taste.
    - Sprinkle with chopped cilantro and any optional toppings you desire, such as crumbled feta cheese, toasted nuts or seeds, or a drizzle of hot sauce.
5. **Serve:**
    - Serve the quinoa breakfast bowls immediately, allowing each person to mix and combine the ingredients to their liking.

Tips:

- **Variations:** Feel free to customize your quinoa breakfast bowl with different vegetables, proteins (like grilled chicken or tofu), or dressings (such as a tahini or yogurt-based dressing).
- **Make-Ahead:** Cook the quinoa ahead of time and store it in an airtight container in the refrigerator. Reheat gently in the microwave or on the stovetop before assembling the breakfast bowls.

- **Nutritional Benefits:** Quinoa is a great source of protein and fiber, making it a nutritious base for your breakfast bowl. The addition of eggs and avocado provides healthy fats and additional protein, while fresh vegetables add vitamins and minerals.

This quinoa breakfast bowl is not only wholesome and nutritious but also versatile and easy to customize according to your preferences. Enjoy this flavorful and satisfying meal to kick-start your day!

Breakfast grilled cheese

Ingredients:

- 4 slices of bread (your choice of bread, such as whole wheat, sourdough, or artisan bread)

- Butter, softened
- 4 slices of cheese (such as cheddar, Swiss, or mozzarella)
- 4 slices of cooked bacon or breakfast sausage patties
- 4 large eggs
- Salt and pepper, to taste
- Optional: sliced tomatoes, avocado, spinach, or other desired toppings

Instructions:

1. **Cook the Eggs:**
   - In a non-stick skillet, melt a small amount of butter over medium heat.
   - Crack the eggs into the skillet and cook them to your preference (scrambled, fried, or poached). Season with salt and pepper to taste. Remove from heat and set aside.
2. **Assemble the Sandwiches:**
   - Heat a large skillet or griddle over medium heat.
   - Butter one side of each slice of bread.
   - Place 2 slices of bread, buttered side down, on the skillet.
   - Layer each slice of bread with a slice of cheese, followed by cooked bacon or breakfast sausage, and then the cooked eggs.
   - If desired, add optional toppings such as sliced tomatoes, avocado, or spinach.
   - Top each sandwich with another slice of bread, buttered side facing up.
3. **Grill the Sandwiches:**
   - Cook the sandwiches on the skillet until the bottom bread slice is golden brown and the cheese begins to melt, about 3-4 minutes.
   - Carefully flip each sandwich with a spatula and cook the other side until golden brown and the cheese is completely melted, another 3-4 minutes.
4. **Serve:**
   - Remove the sandwiches from the skillet and let them cool slightly.
   - Cut each sandwich in half diagonally or serve whole.
   - Serve immediately while warm and enjoy your delicious breakfast grilled cheese!

Tips:

- **Variations:** Customize your breakfast grilled cheese by using different types of cheese, adding vegetables like spinach or sliced tomatoes, or using different proteins such as ham or turkey.
- **Make-Ahead:** You can prepare the components ahead of time (cooked eggs, bacon or sausage) and assemble and grill the sandwiches in the morning for a quick breakfast.
- **Serving Suggestions:** Serve the breakfast grilled cheese with a side of fresh fruit, a small salad, or a cup of soup for a complete and satisfying meal.

This breakfast grilled cheese is a comforting and flavorful option that combines gooey cheese, savory proteins, and eggs in a crispy, buttery sandwich. It's sure to become a favorite for breakfast or brunch!

www.ingramcontent.com/pod-product-compliance
Lightning Source LLC
LaVergne TN
LVHW061945070526
838199LV00060B/3988